JAKE

AN AMERICAN ORIGINAL

VOLUME I

CLIFF GALLANT

Cover Photo: Jake on his Harley arriving home to Portland after his two day straight run from his mountain-top retreat in Ward, Colorado.

Jake Sawyer
Hells Angels Nomads

Jake: An American Original, Vol I

This is a work of memoir and reportage. Facts have been preserved and related truthfully to the best of the author's knowledge.

Unless otherwise credited, photos are the property and copyright of Jake Sawyer.

ISBN: 978-1-950381-28-9

Published by Piscataqua Press
32 Daniel St., Portsmouth NH 03801

www.ppressbooks.com

Printed in the United States of America

AN AMERICAN ORIGINAL

**The Astonishing, Shockingly Violent,
Sex-filled, Often Hilarious
Life Story of Jake Sawyer:**

★An Original Hell's Angel Nomad
★U.S. Army Paratrooper
★Legendary Health and Fitness Trainer to the Elite and
Not So Elite
★Trainer of Award-winning Bodybuilders and Power Lifters
★Arm Wrestling Champion
★Prep School Sports Star
★High Profile Inmate of Notorious State and Federal Prisons
★Ferocious Fighter and Expert Knife Thrower
★Scoundrel
★A Friend to the End

THE MEN THAT DON'T FIT IN

There's a race of men that don't fit in,
A race that can't stay still;
So they break the hearts of kith and kin,
And they roam the world at will.
They range the field and they rove the flood,
And they climb the mountain's crest;
Theirs is the curse of the gypsy blood,
And they don't know how to rest.

If they just went straight they might go far;
They are strong and brave and true;
But they're always tired of the things that are,
And they want the strange and new.

-Robert Service

DEDICATED TO

RALPH "SONNY" BARGER

There he was, the infamous Jake Sawyer, still as rugged and menacing looking as ever, peering intently over the crowd at me as I came out of the library. This can't be, I thought. I'd been in Jake's presence a few times over the years, but I wasn't sure he would remember or be interested in anything about me. He's obviously spotted an acquaintance of his in my vicinity, I said to myself. Maybe an outlaw-biker he rode with, or an old weight-lifting buddy, or it could be some long-lost partner in crime. I'd heard that he was the first Hell's Angel from Maine, and that he'd done serious time in some of the country's most notorious penitentiaries, so maybe he's spotted some luminary from his past that he thought he'd never see on the street again. Or maybe it's that I'm blocking his view of some hot-looking babe he's been after, I thought, and I'll just quickly scoot out of the way. But no, as soon he was sure he'd caught my eye, he gave me a sharp nod of the head by way of communicating to me that I'd be well advised to stand my ground because he and I had an appointment to keep, whether I remembered making it or not.

Jake's always been known for his flamboyant way of dressing, and that day he was wearing a three-cornered Revolutionary War hat with a feather sticking out of it, like one of Ethan Allen's Green Mountain men. As he got closer, I saw that his long hair was dyed different colors on each side, light blue on one side, canary yellow on the other, and what immediately came to mind was how the tough guys in high school would sometimes walk down the sidewalk wearing a girl's kerchief around their necks to draw wise-cracks, then whammo.

"Oh, hi, how ya doin'?" I said, trying to act as relaxed and casual as possible when he planted his heavy black boots, one after the other, directly in front of me. He stood there peering into my eyes, seeming to take the true measure of me. For what reason, I did not know.

The quivering in my stomach was a matter of concern because I knew that if there's anything that riles Hell's Angels as much as snitches do, it's "Tinker-bells." There's a tale in the book *Hell's Angels*, by Hunter Thompson, about some of them hanging a guy from a chandelier by one thumb in the middle of a party because they could see he was nervous around them. One of them saw a little twitch, that scared rabbit look, hearty guffaws ensued, and up the unfortunate fellow went.

They say Jake's nickname in the Hell's Angels was "Bonecrusher," and now here he was, looming over me.

"I know who you are," he began.

"Ya, okay, I ah ..." I said.

"You're a writer!" he yelled. "I've been reading your column in the newspaper with your picture next to it and you're the man I've been looking for! I want my life story written and you're the one who's going to do it!"

Oh no, I thought, here we go again. As it often is with local columnists, readers are always coming up to me in public and telling me that I should write their life story. "It'll be a best seller!" they always say, then they give you a prolonged synopsis of their life that bores you almost to tears, and as they're leaving and waving good-bye they invariably add: "They'll make it into a movie too! No question! We'll split the profits on everything all the way, fifty-fifty!"

But this was Jake Sawyer in front of me now, not some delusional wannabe. How the hell am I going to get out of this? I asked myself. Oh well, I thought, he'll probably talk himself out in one interview session anyway. That's the way it usually is with people and their life stories. I'll just go along with the idea. We'll meet at some bar, and when he's talked himself out, I'll quietly make my exit and he'll forget the whole thing. Sounded like a plan, but then came the barrage, and I knew it might not be that easy.

"I've got a lifetime of stories piled up and I've got to unload them!" he boomed. "Some of them took place in good ol' Portland, and some of them took place in other exotic and equally as beautiful places across our great country! I've been everywhere and I've done everything! I've done things that other people don't even dare to dream of doing! Not only did I become a patch-holding member of the Hell's Angels Motorcycle Club after what is likely the shortest time spent as a prospect in the history of the club, but I was also incarcerated in some of the country's most notorious and dangerous prisons and penitentiaries. But that's not what my life was all about, no sir, not by a long shot. I've also been a prep school sports star, a United States Army Paratrooper, a successful businessman, and a very well-known and respected weight and physical fitness trainer. I've also been a great friend to people in need on many occasions through my life, if that counts for anything. I've been waiting a long time to see it all in one place, sir, and I am eager to tell you fantastic and absolutely true stories about these and other fascinating aspects of my highly unusual life!

"This isn't about bragging or telling outrageous stories, though," he continued, calming down a bit,

VOLUME ONE

"I'm just tired of hearing all these bullshit stories people tell about me and I want to set things straight. If I don't get it out now my whole life will go down as a garbled-up mess and I don't want that. We're after the truth. Because the truth is gonna set us free, man!"

He paused and squinted at me, studying my face to see if I was paying proper attention. I was. I was very ill at ease and a little mystified, but I was definitely paying attention.

"I've been a pirate and a madman," he continued, talking now in a quiet and reflective way, "but I've also been a thinker, and maybe I've even done some good for a few people here and there, at least I hope so." He spread his arms wide and swiveling around to face people passing by on the sidewalk, as if they were filing by just to get a look at him.

"Okay, man, here we go, here's what's behind all this madness," he went on. "My reason for wanting this book written is so that there will be some meaning to my life, and so I'll be able to help other people in some way. I want them to see what a life lived right straight out looks like. Just so that they can apply whatever impressions they might get to their own lives and make the best use of the tremendous talents we've all been given. The whole purpose of this incredible life is to enjoy and appreciate every moment of it, is it not, sir? I don't expect everyone to become outlaw-bikers and commit violent acts, then spend a lot of time behind bars the way I've done. No way, sir. I merely want to help people be all they can be in their own lives. You might not believe it, I'm sure you don't, but I harbor a deep love for my fellow human beings inside the over-developed, extremely muscular chest you're looking at, sir."

He was right, of course, I didn't believe it. I just

stood there with my head hung down a little, blank-faced. It had never even occurred to me that there was anything at all high-minded about Jake Sawyer and I was a bit baffled by what was being played out in front of me.

"I've got no idea how it all balances out, though," he went on, "but maybe seeing it all together in a book will answer that question. Maybe it doesn't even all have to balance out or make any sense, though, who knows? That's a helluva question itself. Some people love me, some people hate me, but nobody knows the truth about me, and maybe they should if they care so friggin' much."

"Yeah, yeah," I said, the way an old buddy would.

"All I know is that the true story has to be told and it better get done pretty soon. I've never been concerned with getting old because I never thought I'd get there, and I don't feel much different than I ever did, but everybody kicks off someday, and ol' Jakie boy is no exception. At least I don't think I'm going to live forever! Maybe I'm wrong, though! Who knows?! It wouldn't be the first time I surprised the hell out of everybody! I was supposed to be dead a long time ago! I've been shot at numerous times, but I was hit only twice, once in the head and once in the chest. I survived both times, obviously, thanks to my guardian angel, who, I'm very grateful to say, has always been with me."

Twirling around theatrically, he broke out in a clownish grin and primped the yellow side of his long hair, preening for a group of businessmen in suits and ties passing by, eliciting good-natured smiles and nods of the head from them, in contrast to the practiced indifference they customarily show to demonstrative street characters. There's something about Jake's carriage, and the look in his eye, that tells men of any stripe not to disrespect the guy, even if he's acting a little silly at the moment.

I threw my head back, looking up into the sky, not knowing how to react to it all. Honestly, I was still pretty taken aback by Jake Sawyer even speaking to me. I'm not the most outgoing guy on the block, after all. I don't get noticed all that much. Now here was Jake Sawyer wanting very badly to tell me the intimate details of his life story. Part of me was kind of aglow with the thought, but another part of me wanted to pivot and run the other way.

He's definitely an interesting and very entertaining guy, I was thinking, and it would be cool to hear about his time in the Hell's Angels and his experiences in big-time prisons, but did I really want to have to listen to him tell about the time he beat this and that guy to within an inch of their lives in a bar fight one night, and for no other reason but that he could? And do I want to hear the details of all the two-bit robberies he's probably pulled off, where small business people had their hard-earned life savings stolen from them, and might even have gotten seriously roughed up, or maybe ended up buried in a gravel pit up in northern Maine somewhere? I don't want any of that crap in my head myself, so why would a reader? All things weighed out and considered, it was my heartfelt desire to just move on, but I didn't quite know how to hit him with that.

Becoming aware of my discomfort, I suppose, and wanting to lighten things up a bit, he smiled and leaned closer to me. "I do kind of get that time is moving on, though, if you know what I mean," he said, patting the light blue side of his head. "If I didn't do anything to it, my damn hair would grow out gray and who wants to see ol' Jakie boy with gray hair?"

Two teen-aged girls tee-heed as they went by, thoroughly delighting him.

"You like it? You like it?" he called after them gaily, running his fingers through the hair on both sides of his head.

"Yessss ... it's sooo beautiful!" they answered back, falling over each other giggling and blushing, charmed by a master.

As they continued down the sidewalk, looking back and waving good-bye to him, he smiled broadly and laughed, savoring the moment, then lowered his head and stood there musing to himself, far away somewhere. Before long he snapped back to the matter at hand, though, even more animated than before.

"I've done it all! My life's been one helluva story and I want it out there!"

I stood there looking at him, slowly nodding, trying to calculate what had been just presented to me, a bit overwhelmed by it all.

"I've done some amazing things in my life, but they're all just things I've done, they're not who I am. Who I am is a former member of the Hell's Angels Motorcycle Club and I will carry that honor with me to my grave! When I found the Hell's Angels, I found my true family! Nothing I've ever done compares to that! Nothing! Sonny Barger is the Messiah and I am one of his disciples! He is the ultimate leader of men and I would follow him into a blast furnace! My Hell's Angels brothers, who I will always love, will definitely be in the book! They will damn sure be in the book!"

As if I had said they wouldn't be. I wouldn't do that. I wouldn't.

He stood there on the sidewalk looking intently into my face, not saying anything more for the moment. I could see that he was collecting his thoughts for some kind of final surge, though. He had something important to add and he wanted to get it just right. When he finally spoke, it was in a much more measured tone than before. It was obviously important to him that I understand him very clearly. I had never thought that Jake Sawyer would give a damn either way how I felt about anything, never mind what I thought about him, but he obviously did, and the words started pouring out of him.

"I know you probably think I'm nothing but a raving, self-obsessed, violent, dumb-ass outlaw-biker with a huge chip on his shoulder, and I am, sort of," he said, nodding his head in acknowledgment and chuckling a bit. "But I'm also a very conscientious and fair-minded individual who's deeply in love with life and with his fellow human beings. My main reason for wanting this book written, sir, is that I believe it will be of interest to the great number of people who are looking for some answers concerning how they might live their own lives. I've never shrunk away from a thing in my whole life, and maybe my story will help someone or other do something they're afraid of doing. It's the fear that stops us, man, not the thing itself. If you face your fears by going right straight for the gusto every time, life becomes a great feast. I've always done everything with great passion, and I've loved every minute of it, even the bad times. I've gone right straight for the most exciting thing I can find to do at the moment every friggin' time and it's always worked out in the end. I came up smilin' every time! Life is one grand celebration of being here and being exactly who you are, man! And that's what I want to turn people on to! Let's have at it!"

I still wasn't sold, but I found myself smiling and

mulling things over. I've always taken a great interest in the local scene, and I'd always been fascinated by Jake Sawyer and his doings, true, but did I really want to commit to writing a book about him? What he had just said about his motives for wanting his life story written weren't concepts I would've associated with Jake Sawyer, and that intrigued me, for sure, but it's also true that the guy's a notorious brawler and all-around law-breaker. Do I really want to spend time alone with him? What happens if we're getting along then all of a sudden, things go south? What the hell happens if he thinks I've crossed him in some way? What if I write about him in a way he doesn't like? What if he wants me to write things I know damn well can't be true? Or what if I reveal things that could be used as evidence against him? He'll hunt me down for sure when he gets out, no question, I said to myself. It'll fester with him the whole time he's in there. My life will be a living hell, I stood there thinking, all the while trying to appear relaxed in his presence. He seemed to sense my unease and hit me with another volley.

"Mister man, I'm going to tell you some things that are gonna knock your friggin' socks off! I'm going to lay it all out, the complete truth, from the beginning to what's going on in my life right now! You're going to get it right from the horse's ass that lived it and you're going to be the one who gets the real story out there! And I've got pictures of it all! I've been preparing for this moment for my whole life, man, and here we are!"

Oh no, I moaned to myself, shaking my head. What about all the other writing I had planned, projects that involve relating to normal people and doing healthy, wholesome things?

"You might even find, sir," he continued, with a

tone of confidentiality intended to draw me in, "that there are things about the crazy-assed individual in front of you that people know nothing about. Things that have nothing to do with my violent bad-boy side. Other-worldly things. I have had experiences through-out my life that have been both wondrous and deeply mysterious, and I look forward to sharing them with you."

In the almost fifty years that I had known of Jake Sawyer, never had I gained the slightest impression that there was anything sensitive or spiritually in-clined about him, and I was a little stunned. It was becoming apparent, though, that the man hadn't spent his life beating people up just for the hell of it and robbing mom and pop corner stores for spending money. There's obviously some depth to him, I was thinking, he's definitely not your run-of-the-mill, in-and-out of jail tough guy. He smiled when he saw the glint in my eye.

"Yeah, okay, Jake, a book, huh?" I said.

We nodded our heads at one another, by way of closing the deal, made an appointment to meet, and that was that. He, not that surprisingly, had one more thing to say, though.

"You have to remember that I was there, and that I've got my own way of telling things. That's just who I am. Sometimes I'm going to have to run wild and get it out there right from my guts and straight from the heart. I've waited a long time for this, and I damned sure want to get it right. For better or worse, it's got to be good and true and honest and me all the way."

"Yup, okay, Jake." I said.

"I've also got something to tell you" he said. "I decided not to get into it until I knew whether you had the balls to take on this project, but here you go."

Me? Jake Sawyer's talking about me? A guy with balls? After that, both he and I knew he had me all the way.

"When we get together to talk," he said, "the first thing I'm going to do is tell you about something I've never told anyone. I'm going to confess to something I did. It's something I've been carrying with me forever, and if I don't get it out it's going to rot inside me, and I won't rest in peace when that great and glorious day comes when I get stuffed into a pine box. I just wanted to let you know something was coming, just so you'll know and won't get too flipped out by it when it comes down.

"So here we go!" he yelled, "we're going to tell the people a story that's gonna blow their friggin' minds! And it's gonna be fifty-fifty all the way! Book, movie, whatever, we split the proceeds and all the glory thereafter fifty-fifty all the way!"

Oh, damn, I muttered to myself. What the hell have I gotten myself into?

ONE

There I was, clumping up the stairs to Jake Sawyer's apartment at ten in the morning, chuckling at myself for even being there. C'mon, I thought, he won't even be home, and even if he is, he'll still be partying with the same outlaw-biker buddies and wild women he's been out raising hell with for who knows how many days and nights. All I could think of was them all laughing their drunk, stoned-at-ten-in-the-morning asses off at me standing there with my notebook tucked under my arm trying to explain to Jake why I'm there.

When I saw that his door was ajar, and I couldn't hear any partying going on inside, I immediately suspected that he had gone out and left the door open on purpose. A guy at a bar once told me that Jake likes to set traps for people. It's one of the ways he has of deciding who's a friend, who's an enemy, and who doesn't matter either way. He'll spot some big tough looking guy coming towards him on the street, for instance, and immediately start staring him down. If the guy returns his stare instead of nervously looking away, Jake smiles and gives him a little nod, then just before they get to one another, he drops a wad of bills behind him on the sidewalk without the guy seeing him do it. If the guy goes by him and quickly picks the money up and pockets it, Jake runs him down and beats the crap out of him. But if the guy picks the money up and yells after him, Jake breaks out in a big smile, walks over to the guy, shakes his hand vigorously, takes the money from him, hands him back half of it, then looks him right straight in the eye and says: "Fifty-fifty all the way." Which in tough guy talk means that from then on you have each other's ass covered, no matter what. Most of the men Jake meets that way had their minds completely blown by Jake at that very first meeting, and from then on will fight alongside him anywhere, anytime, whatever the cause or reason, for the rest of their lives, the guy at the bar told me.

Okay, so I figure that I'm looking at the door-left-ajar trap. Could be that he comes around the corner, finds me breaking into his apartment, and I'm dog meat. Or maybe somehow or other I'll pass with flying colors, and who knows what abundance might flow from that? Anyway, I stood at arm's length from the door then reached out and rapped once, very lightly.

His booming voice reverberated from deep inside somewhere.

"Come in! Enter, sir! That's why it's open! Just keep going until you get to where the booming male voice is coming from and that's where I'll be!"

I was ready for rubbish piled up everywhere, smells, beer bottles strewn around, buddies passed out on the couch, panties thrown in a corner, that kind of thing. But no, as I entered and walked down the short hall toward where his voice had come from, it immediately became apparent that I had seriously prejudged Mr. Sawyer. Rarely have I witnessed such domestic order, particularly on the part of a male living alone. Turns out that Jake Sawyer is a meticulous housekeeper and really knows how to put a living space together. Interesting photos and posters all over the walls, various artistic and historical items on shelves and propped up in the corners, a nice variety of potted plants here and there, and even a sophisticated-looking telescope set up on a tripod in front of his living room window to better take in the terrific view he has of Casco Bay and the Fore River.

"How ya doin'!" he yelled when I got to the living room, springing up out of his chair and shaking my hand. Grasp his hand firmly, but not too firmly, I remember thinking to myself, firmly and confidently, and look him straight in the eye.

His commanding presence and deep voice gave me that tightening of the stomach I hated myself for, but I somehow managed to hold my ground. There I was, back in basic training, but now the First Sargeant was a freshly showered and shaved, extremely fit senior citizen outlaw-biker wearing a white ruffled colonial-style shirt, form-fitting jeans, and highly polished black motorcycle boots.

"Thought I'd dress for the occasion," he said, chuckling. "I've been waiting a long time for this day and I wanted to do it up right."

That's when it started to really sink in me that he was taking this a lot more seriously than I had imagined. I had had my doubts, but at this point I knew that he was on a mission to share all he had seen and done with the whole wide world.

"Have a seat!" he commanded, with a wide smile and a sweeping gesture to a comfortable-looking chair placed directly across from and within easy hearing distance of another one just like it.

So there we were, sitting looking at one another, each waiting for the other to say something. I really didn't know where to start, not knowing at this point exactly what he had in mind, but I was pretty sure asking him about his early childhood wouldn't be a good move. Can you imagine? I was thinking he'd probably jump up and throw me out of the place if I opened with that kind of thing, so I decided to ask him about the large photo up on the wall behind him, of him in the prime of his youth, straddling a motorcycle and wearing the most happy, confident, and fully contented smile I think I've ever seen on anyone in my life.

"That particular photo was taken in the summer of 1966, sir," he answered, "just after I had become a patch-holding member of the Hell's Angels Motorcycle Club. The broad smile has directly to do with the fact that when I became a patch-holding member of the Hell's Angels I had met my destiny in life. I had finally connected with my true family and I was with them at the time this picture was taken, so what's not to smile about? Oh, I should mention that at the time the picture was taken I was out on bail awaiting trial on a series of felony charges that would most likely keep me in prison until I was an old man, if I even got out then. But the probability of going to prison soon wasn't even on my mind when that picture was taken, to tell you the truth. All that mattered to me was that I had become a patch-holding member of the Hell's Angels that summer, and that made it the best period of my life, no matter what else was going on.

"But let us proceed with the mission, sir!" he boomed, with a hearty laugh and an enthusiastic clap of his hands. "Exactly how would you like to begin?"

"Well, Jake," I said, haltingly, "usually life stories start with people talking about their early childhood, but I ..."

He interrupted me before I could finish. My reflexive reaction was to think he was going to call me a pussy and tell me to pack up my pad and pencil and get the hell out of there. I was even kind of inching forward on the chair, ready to comply as quickly as possible. Imagine asking Jake Sawyer to tell you about his early childhood! He's got me up here to talk about his time in the Hell's Angels, all the prisons he's been in, what he did to get there, and all the lawless, sexually depraved, and violent things he's done in his life, now here I am asking him to tell me about things that happened when he was a little boy.

How wrong I was, though. He was all for it.

"Yes! Of course! That's where it all starts! Our early childhood! One of the very main absolutely at the center reasons for wanting to get this book written is that I want to make a confession about something I did in my early adolescence, and if we don't talk about my early childhood you won't know what led up to it, and how it made me into the man I am today! I've never told anybody about it before! As much as I wanted to, I never did, not to any friend, cell mate, or to any woman, whether I loved her or not, but today I'm going to tell you!"

Here it comes, I thought to myself. He's going to tell me about some gruesome crime he committed that there's no statute of limitations on. And he might even tell me where the shallow grave is. So then I'll know, and I'll be an accessory after the fact, or maybe even an accomplice, depending on whose story they believe.

"I'm going to tell you about my early childhood by relating it to some later stages of my life," he began. "We'll play a little forward and backwards kind of game, if you don't mind. That picture you asked about on the wall behind me, of me on my Harley Davidson 74, says it all. Please take a good look at it, sir, because it captures who I was then, who I was as a kid, and who I am right now. Not one damn thing has changed about me!

"One of my earliest memories is straddling a vehicle at four or five years old and riding the hell out of it. The year was 1942 or 1943 and World War Two was still going on. The vehicle in question didn't run on petrol, of course, it ran on kid power. It was one of those extra-special, heavy-duty metal riding trucks that you make go by kicking your legs back. It had 'Made in America' written on it and back in those days that meant that it was made with great pride and integrity and was built to last forever. I was the latest of three generations of first-born Sawyer males to own that toy truck. I remember my father and grandfather chuckling about how much fun they had on it as kids. Somehow, I don't think they'd put it through its paces quite to the degree I did, though. I could make that thing go like hell and I absolutely loved the thrill of it. My mother saw pretty early on that inside the house was not the place for this to be happening, though, so it wasn't long before the toy truck and I were liberated to the backyard. I remember ramming around out there like I was in a wild-ass demolition derby, bashing the hell out of imaginary cars and trucks all day long. I didn't get off that thing until my legs were absolutely exhausted and I felt completely satisfied that I had destroyed everything I had come up against."

Most people remember things like the first book they read as a child, or maybe the first time they went to the beach, I was thinking, but Jake remembers the first time he rode on a vehicle destroying things.

"Let me tell you about the old man and me," he continued, surprising the hell out of me, in that I was still under the misconception that I'd have to somehow coax such things out of him.

"I loved him, and I think he loved me," he continued, "but we were exact opposites and had a piss poor relationship. I was born a warrior and he was born a nice guy. His natural desire was to make me into a copy of himself, though, because he wanted what was best for me and he couldn't envision a better life for me than the one he had led. His father was a very successful business owner and was a well-respected man in the community, and my father had an ex-cellent relationship with him. My grandfather not only instilled a lot of admirable character traits in my father, he also paved the way through life for him in many different ways, including buying him a new Cadillac convertible to drive back and forth to Deering High School in his senior year."

That's a good way to improve your chances of getting a date for the Senior prom, I thought to myself.

"I'm sure it comes as a great surprise to you, sir, but yours truly is descended from a long line of well-known and accomplished people. I have always taken a great interest in history, and I have learned that my ancestors were some of the original settlers of the area and played a large part in its development.

"When Sir Fernando Gorges, an English nobleman who owned a vast tract of land in the area, sent his son to inspect and report to him on his holdings in the year 1654, he hired an ancestor of mine, a Major Norton, who was a highly respected retired officer in the King's army, to accompany his son on his inspection tour of the wild, extremely dangerous wilderness that was at that time called the Province of Maine.

"Out of gratitude for having protected his son as well as he did under such extreme circumstances, Sir Gorges awarded Major Norton a thousand acres of land located at the southern tip of the province, in what today is York County, and Major Norton built what was the second home in that region. He evidently wasn't the stay-at-home type, though, and at some point he got into a skirmish with a band of hostile Pequot Indians at the mouth of the Connecticut River, and met his fate. He was well on his way to routing the enemy all on his own, when the gun powder he kept in a powder bag on his hip was hit by a spark and caught fire. Unfortunately, he was blinded by the smoke and was overrun by the Indians. The Indians later said he fought ferociously even after being blinded, and that they didn't want to harm him, out of respect for his great courage, but they had no choice because he absolutely refused to surrender and was continuing to ferociously attack them.

A descendant of a long line of Sawyers that goes back to some of the original settlers of Maine and New Hampshire, Jake's ancestors include Benjamin Sawyer, for whom Sawyer's Rock, in Conway, New Hampshire, was named.

"Then there was Jot Sawyer, a privateer, and sometimes pirate, who operated in the area before and during the War of 1812. He was hired by Asa Clapp, the most successful merchant of the time, to be the 'muscle' in his very lucrative shipping operations. Jot got a crew of hardened seafaring men together – evidently he had my talent for getting other males to do his bidding – and it was him and his men who made the shipping channels along the coast of northern New England safe for navigation by merchant trading ships.

"Oh, and I can't forget John Sawyer! In the year 1719 John became the first ferryman on the banks of the Fore River, before there was a bridge between South Portland and Portland. Everyone in both towns got to know John over the years, of course, and he became a popular individual. It might interest you to know, sir, that Sawyer Street, which is today the main thoroughfare running through the city of South Portland and the neighboring town of Cape Elizabeth, was named for my illustrious ancestor, John Sawyer!

"What you have to know, sir," Jake continued, "is that my family owned a very well-known and respected Maine clothing manufacturing company by the name of Sawyer-Barker that had been in the family for three generations. It was located in the center of downtown Portland, on Center Street, just off Congress. The most well-known item in Sawyer-Barker's inventory was Johnson Pants, which were made to protect a man from the elements in the worst Maine winters. They were made so well they'd often last for twenty years or more and they were very popular throughout the State of Maine. Think of all those old time Mainers wearing the same pants for twenty years!"

"I'd rather not," I said, eliciting a big belly laugh from him.

Jake, on the right, at age 5 in 1943, with his friends to the end Dana and Ronnie, proudly displaying their Indian war paint.

By Staff Photographer Bridson
AFTER ALL THOSE YEARS—It was farewell to the job after 59 years on it Friday for Albert A. Austin, 75, right. He's shown shaking hands with Stewart E. Sawyer, treasurer of the Sawyer-Barker Company, as he left to start his retirement from the firm.

Jake's father, Stewart E. Sawyer, bidding a fond farewell and expressing a sincere thank you to a fifty-nine year employee of the Sawyer-Barker Company. At some point in time, Jake was moved to print "Good Man" on his father's shirt sleeve.

JAKE

"Anyway, Sawyer-Barker was one of those very old Maine companies that took a great deal of pride in their products. The company also fostered a very personal and responsible relationship with their employees. This was before there were unions, but my family always made sure people were paid well and were taken care of in time of need anyway. I took a great deal of pride in the company myself and worked there for a while in my teen years. As was the family custom, I started out doing menial jobs, with the intent being that I would rise up through the ranks like other members of my family had, but it wasn't happening with me. I always did my job well, and all the workers liked me, and I liked them, but I was far too much of a free spirit to be anybody's boss for very long and everybody knew it, including my father and me.

"Because my father was a well-respected guy and was known for having the best interests of other people in mind, it's no surprise that he got talked into running for political office. From as early as I can remember, there was always a lot of political hubbub going on in our house. I'd often come home to a living room full of strangers. People I didn't know would be going into our refrigerator to get some ice for their drink, that kind of thing. My father was elected to a few terms as City Councilor and ended up serving as Chairman of the City Council, but that stuff meant nothing to me. I was definitely missing him in my life. All I wanted was to hear him say he loved me, but he never said it. He was too busy being everything to everybody else, so there you go."

I could never have imagined hearing Jake Sawyer say he missed having his father say he loved him. There you go, indeed.

VOLUME ONE

"So I saw and heard a lot of the hypocrisy and self-serving policy making that went on in town, hatched right there in my family's living room. My father was a good man, though, in his own way. Kind and considerate, and very well meaning. Did a lot of good for a lot of people. It's not his fault he ended up with an asshole for a son."

Jake Sawyer comes from a prominent South Portland family. Damn. Who would've thought?

"One day, I heard my father and his friends talking about Hitler and what a bad man he was," Jake continued, "and I immediately became obsessed with the idea of defeating fucking Hitler all by myself. It's all I could think of, and I was only six-years old. My father and his friends were confused as hell by my intensity. They just didn't get me. Play-it-safe guys like them never do. I've been experiencing it my whole life. Anyway, somehow or other I had heard that one way to help defeat Hitler was by donating metal to the Salvation Army, so when one of their trucks came around the neighborhood picking up items, I ran out and gave my toy truck to them. I've told you how much I loved that truck, but it made me happy as hell to think of the Salvation Army melting it down into a big bullet to shoot up Hitler's ass. The whole thing really confused and hurt my father, to tell the truth, because that truck had been handed down the line to me from my grandfather, and I obviously loved it, but now here I was, giving it away. It really bothered his friends too, because they knew how much I loved that truck, and that I'd be willing to part with it like that worried them a lot. If I got mad at them like I was mad at friggin' Adolph Hitler, who was way over in Germany, what the hell would I do to them in my own goddamn living room? And, you know, they were right to ask themselves that question, come to think of it!"

Jake laughed heartily this, and I chuckled along with him, but inside I was kind of worried about that six-year-old kid, the way his father and his friends must have been, I guess. After a moment, he calmed down and continued.

"As time went on, I graduated from ramming around the backyard in my toy truck to riding my bike around the neighborhood like a bat out of hell, and it wasn't long before I had a rounded up bunch of kids and we became masters of all we surveyed. I was always trying to be the fastest one, of course. My house was on a hill and I had a speedometer on my bike, and I remember the exact downhill speed I got up to: 32 miles per hour. Which, come to think of it, is probably the equivalent of the 171.4 miles per hour I got my Boss Hoss motorcycle up to about fifty years later, when I set the unofficial motorcycle land speed record up near Fryeburg, Maine. I'll tell you all about that in great detail when we get to that point in our discussion, sir, but for now let's stick to my misspent youth.

"I'd challenge the other kids to keep up with me going down the hill and we'd often end up crashing at the bottom and coming home with scratches and bruises all over us. As you might imagine, I wasn't very popular with my friends' parents, but there you go. I've always got kind of a perverse pleasure out of tweaking the noses of authority figures anyway, and I've always liked acting out the most when I could patch together a band of eager followers. I felt so supercharged when I was leading that gang of ten-year-old desperadoes on a wild bike ride that I can recall the feeling as if it was yesterday.

"It wasn't all me, me, and more me, though, not by

any means. The pack is what really mattered to me, just like it was with the Hell's Angels years later. When I was a kid, I didn't feel connected with my home life. As a kid, and as a grown man, I was always trying to make up for my poor relationship with my father by bonding with male friends. One for all, all for one, you know how that goes.

"When I was a kid riding my bike with the pack I was always looking back to see if everyone was keeping up, and if someone wasn't I'd circle back and get them fired up to get up there and take the lead and I was amazed at how often they'd do just that. That was about the time I started to realize that I had a great natural talent for inspiring other males and getting them to do my bidding."

I nodded to myself in affirmation of that one.

"I've got a little story about just that very thing, sir, involving one of my Hell's Angels brothers named Big Al, but we won't get into it at this point. Please stop trying to get me off subject!"

I looked over at him a little sheepishly, not quite sure if he was kidding or not. He looked down at the floor, though, frowning and shaking his head ruefully, as if he knew he had a long ways to go with me.

"Anyway, sir," he resumed, "keeping to the matter at hand, one weird detail of my bicycle riding career is that, out of nowhere, I got the urge to paint my bike bright red, which, of course, as I found out years later, is the predominant color of the Hell's Angels Motorcycle Club logo and paraphernalia. Things connected to the Hell's Angels have always occurred throughout my life, before and after I bonded with my brothers.

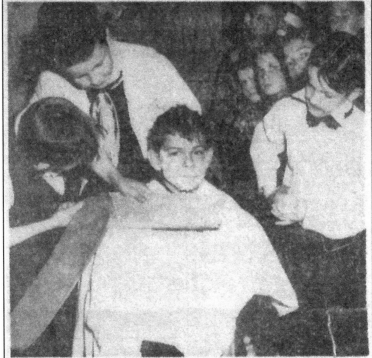

Big Cub Scout Carnival-Circus Held In South Portland Armory

By Sunday Telegram Photographer Roberts

OPERATION WHISKER—A close shave was the order of the day for these four members of Cub Scout Pack 24, First Congregational Church, who coincidentally combined a barber shop and first aid booth at the carnival-circus in South Portland Saturday. Wielding the king size straight edge is Carleton Hackett. Jonathan Sawyer is the victim, and a willing one at that since the lather was whipped cream. Supervising is David Rice, rear, and Ronald Dyer, right. *1948*

A 1948 newspaper clipping.

Friday, June 16, 1950

PROGRAMME

Duo—Vale of Song	*Rolfe-Orem*
CYNTHIA TRAFTON, MISS DOWNS	
The Chime Clock	*Erb*
ROBERT EVANS, JR.	
Old MacDonald's Farm	*Arr. Aaron*
PATRICIA HUNTER	
Gay Butterflies	*Beetz*
RENEE BOUDREAU	
Punch and Judy March	*Lake*
JONATHAN SAWYER	
Duo—The Wood Nymph's Harp	*Rea-Carter*
JANET FARLEY, MISS DOWNS	
Lucita (Spanish Dance)	*Dunlap*
BEVERLEY HOLT	
The Haunted House	*Stevens*
PATRICIA DAVIDSON	
Winter Winds	*Robinson*
ELLEN SAWIN	
Castanets	*Rebe*
JANET FARLEY	
Duo—Dance of the Sunbeams	*Cadman*
DIANE MOORES, MISS DOWNS	

The piano recital "Programme" of a performance by the pupils of Miss Ocy L. Downs. Jake says playing piano didn't work out for him, but that he did acquire a life-long love of dancing from having taken lessons at the Dorothy Mason School of Dance, and was called "Jake the Dancer" by his Hell's Angels brothers, and later owned and operated a corner variety store in Portland he named Dancer's Variety.

JAKE

They have occurred with such regularity that I have developed the habit of taking them for granted, as a matter of fact. Meeting my Hell's Angels brothers was my destiny. It was ordained from the moment of my conception and there have been clear signs of it throughout my life. What does it matter that the paint I used to paint my bike was house paint? Hey, I was just a kid and I didn't know any better. But I sure as hell liked the looks of that bright red bike – and I didn't know until years later that the reason I liked it so much is because they're the Hell's Angels colors!"

When I looked over at Jake and saw his far-away smile, I got my first hint that the outlaw-biker culture is a whole lot deeper than I knew it to be.

"Okay," he said after a moment, "now I'm going to get serious about this little project we've got going and tell you about my mother, which is where we really get into my head, like the way it is with anybody else, I guess. In the end, ol' Jakie boy isn't that much different than anybody else, is he?"

I didn't know whether he wanted confirmation of that, or whether he wanted me to disagree, so I just kept looking down at my notebook, scribbling away.

"My mother was the most important person in my life," he continued, choosing to overlook my silence, "and she's the one person in my life I have loved unconditionally, no questions asked, and will forever and ever. She's gone now and I miss her every day. I loved her with all my heart, and I had a very deep respect for her. She gave me inner strength and self-discipline, and I'll always be grateful to her for whatever scrap of character I happen to have. Respect is something you earn, you don't get it just for who you are, and my mother most definitely earned mine."

VOLUME ONE

THE EVENT THAT SHAPED A LIFE

"We are at the point, sir," he said, "where I am going tell you about the event I referred to when we first met on the street, the event that shaped my life. It has directly to do with my relationship with my mother, and the reason I'm free to tell the story now, as I said, is that she's gone and it can't hurt her. This thing I want to get off my chest has to do with how my mother and I became friends, not just mother and son, but friends, and how I discovered who I am and how I was going to live my life from then on. Just like I told you when we met on the street, man, I've never told the story I'm about to tell you to anyone, not my Hell's Angels brothers, not any blood relatives, cell mates, friends, or any woman, whether I loved her or not, but now I'm going to tell it to you!"

I had a sudden impulse to jump up and run out of there before it was too late, but something told me that I couldn't live with myself thereafter if I did.

"Some background information might provide some context for the incident I'm about to tell you about, sir. To begin with, you have to be aware that I grew up as a little rich kid. We lived in a very nice neighbor-hood just a couple blocks from the seashore. I had all the advantages, but I knew that not everyone had what I had. When I saw some teenage puke up the street taking his golf clubs out of the trunk of his daddy's car, my instinct was to go over and shove a nine-iron up his smug little ass, for instance. I really don't know where those feelings came from, I really don't. All I can say is that it's the attitude I've had right from the very beginning.

"The summer after eighth grade, my father sent me

to a boarding caddie school at The Oyster Harbor Country Club, down in Cape Cod, Massachusetts. He said it was to give me a taste of hard work and to teach me how to get along with people. I was just a skinny kid at that point, and I spent a gruesome three months lugging very heavy golf bags for guys who had never done a real day's work in their lives and tipped me less than they spent on a drink in the clubhouse. I finished up that summer one very angry young man, with not a lot of money to show for all my hard work and kissing rich guys' asses all summer long. As much as I was pissed off at those shallow run-of-the-mill pricks, though, I was even more pissed-off at my father for sending me to the friggin' place. He thought the experience would teach me some valuable lessons in life, and it did, but they weren't the lessons he had in mind. The number one thing I learned from the experience is that you get absolutely nothing out of kissing people's asses and playing by their rules. Ever since then, the only one I've tried to impress is myself. I've lived my life playing by my own rules, and that's just the way it is.

"My mother was not comfortable in my father's way of life either, so we had something in common. We both wanted more out of life than my father was capable of giving us. He was a great guy, but there was just no passion in him. Even when I was a little kid, I saw the disappointment in my mother's eyes when she looked at him. I felt sorry for her and I always ached to do something to help her. She started drinking heavily and watching her deteriorate was torture for me. It started when I was about ten years old. At first, she started getting a little tipsy before my father's political cronies arrived so she could be the fun host-ess, but then as time went on, I'd come home and find her passed out on the floor. It was killing me.

"The drinking wasn't all that was going on, though. It feels shitty even saying it, but after a while I'd come home and find strange men in the living room drinking with my mother when my father wasn't there. It made me sick. My life became pure torture. I was friggin' angry all the time. My father must have known what was going on with my mother, too. He just didn't know what to do about it, I guess, and was just hoping it would just go away by itself.

"The whole thing came to a head one day when I came home from school and was making a sandwich in the kitchen and listening to some guys in the living room with my mother telling raunchy jokes, etc. They were having a high jolly ol' good time. My mother was a very attractive woman, and in an unhappy marriage, so you know how that goes. I was only fourteen years old, but I can hear them partying like it was happening right now. The whole scene filled me with such revulsion I couldn't stand it anymore.

"I had one of those short paring knives in my hand, and I remember very clearly how I stood there in the kitchen just holding it, listening to one of them telling a fucking disgusting joke. He was a very big man, and I'd been wanting to confront him for a long time, but I was afraid to. Then it happened. It was one of those things that you sort of just watch yourself doing. You know what I mean? All of a sudden I found myself running like a madman into the living room with that knife held out in front of me like a friggin' sword, screaming my head off at the guy telling the joke to get the fuck out of there before I slit his fucking throat! My mother screamed and the guy jumped up from the couch and spilled his drink, but there was no slowing me down! I was across the room and on that bastard before he knew what hit him!

"There were two other guys in the room, sitting in easy chairs on opposite sides of the couch, and neither one of them moved a friggin' bit when they saw me going after their buddy. At first, I went for the guy's gut. I was going to lance him straight on, right through the belly button, like fuckin' Zorro, but he fell back on the couch just in time and I didn't quite reach him. That didn't slow me down, though. I figured I'd just lean in and stab at whatever part of him I could make contact with. He saw what my intent was, though, so he rolled to the side and propelled himself up off the couch and made a break for the door. That's when I got the bastard good! Stabbed him once in the thigh as he was getting up, and once in the right cheek of his ass just before he got to the door! That one went in pretty good! Oh, what a tremendous feeling that gave me! He yelped like hell and jumped about two feet in the air! Seeing him up in the air holding onto his ass where the blood was spurting out was so absolutely glorious and satisfying! When he came down and hit the floor he was yowling like a bastard! He made it out the door some damn quick too!

"One of the most memorable moments of my life was standing at the doorway clutching the bloody knife and watching that guy running in great panic across the lawn holding onto his ass with blood running down his pant leg! 'If I ever see you here again I will slit your fucking throat!' I screamed at him! Never in my life have I ever felt such complete and total vindication and power!"

"So after he was gone what did you do, Jake?" I asked, looking over at him slack-jawed with my eyes popped open.

VOLUME ONE

"I AM THE ANGEL FROM HELL!!"

"Those other two guys were gone and the house was quiet except for the sound of my mother sobbing. I stopped long enough to comfort her as much as I could, then I took off. I ran into the backyard, jumped over the old stone wall that ran around our property, then ran through the neighborhood with blood all over my hands and ended up at Dana Beach, which is a nearby ocean inlet which neighborhood people have been going to forever. As soon as I got there, I spotted a large rock sitting there in the sand that my friends and I had played King of the Mountain on when we were kids, and I immediately ran down and jumped up on it and yelled: 'I AM THE ANGEL FROM HELL!'

"Please keep in mind that this was fifteen years before I had even heard of the Hell's Angels! Where those words came from that day, I do not know! I was screaming out my destiny and I had absolutely no idea of that at the time!"

AFTER THE STABBING

"I jumped down from the rock, washed the blood of my hands in the water, then got on the wooded trail that led to my pal Phil's house. I was very thirsty, so I told Phil that I had been playing football with some friends of ours and needed a drink. Phil was three years older than I was, and he had introduced me to *Playboy* magazine and other grown-up delights, so when he grinned and said he had some hard cider his father had somehow acquired, I was all for it.

JAKE

"So there we were, leaning back in a couple of lawn chairs, seated at the edge of the thirty-foot high cliff that overlooks the glistening waters of Portland Harbor, sipping exceptionally smooth and potent hard cider, happy as hell. I recall those moments sitting there with Phil that day as one of the happiest experiences of my life. I had been dreaming of killing that guy for a long time, but he was a very big man and I was afraid of him. You have to remember that I was a scrawny young teenager at that time. I hadn't started lifting weights yet and was somewhat lacking in self-confidence. But I had thrust my fear aside and attacked him! I had taken my biggest enemy in the adult world head on and sent him on his fucking way holding onto his ass and screaming for his life!

"The way I looked at it, I was David defeating Goliath, and I was so full of confidence that I didn't give a damn what was going to happen when I got home. After I said my jolly good-byes to my buddy Phil, I walked to my house smiling all the way. I didn't care whether I was in serious trouble or not. I had never been so happy in my life and I laughed at the thought of any punishment I might receive, including possibly being sent to some kind of youth detention center.

"As soon as I walked through the door, though, I realized that I was not in any kind of trouble. My mother and father were sitting together in the living room merrily chatting away like it was just another day on Deake Street!

"Oh, man! Little did they know the kind of life their little Jakie boy was now set up to lead!

"Anyway, we didn't have any more trouble with unwanted afternoon male visitors after that little episode. My mother turned her life around big time after the incident, too. I guess it was the immensity of what

happened. Unbelievably, my mother and I never exchanged one word about the incident, and I have every
reason to believe that my father never found out a
thing about it. Everything went unspoken between my
mother and me. The big thing was that she knew that
she finally had a man in her life, and that's all that
mattered. I was very pleased at the way I'd find her
looking at me now and then. She knew she now had a
man who not only loved her, but who would stand up
for her, no matter what. She finally had someone in
her life she could depend on and respect. From the
time of that incident, she just kind of ignored my
father and got on with her own life. She got straight,
became very successful as a real estate investor, and
was in the society pages all the time. Not as my
father's wife, but on her own."

He looked over at me across the room scribbling
away and smiled.

"You don't know how good it feels to finally tell
someone that story I just told you," he said, leaning
back in his chair, and sitting there for a moment with
his hands folded behind his head, quietly looking up
at the ceiling, savoring the moment by repeating what
he'd told me earlier about having kept the incident to
himself for so long.

"There have been a lot of people who've tried to get
into my head, my friend: women I've been involved
with, good male friends of mine, court-appointed
shrinks. I've often led them to believe that they've got
me all figured out, but I've always smiled to myself,
because I knew something that they didn't have any
knowledge of whatsoever.

"I developed the habit of taking my fate in my own
hands ever since that incident. Now all I want to do is
tell the people what a life lived right straight out looks

like, so maybe they'll be able to wring a little more pleasure and satisfaction out of their own lives. So, here we go, huh? You with me?"

"Yeah ... yeah, okay, Jake, see you next time," I said, throwing my pen down onto my notebook, and I knew from his impish grin that I was in for one helluva ride.

Jake, pictured on the front of a calendar, one year before the event that set the course of his life.

TWO

The door to his apartment was ajar, the way it was when I arrived for our first interview, but this time instead of knocking timidly and being ready to make a quick getaway, I rapped solidly and yelled out: "How ya doin' Jake!" and just walked right in, the way an ol' buddy would.

"Welcome, my friend!" he boomed.

There I was, ol' buddies with a guy who was a member of the most violent chapter of the Hell's Angels and spent a good part of his adult life incarcerated in various lock-ups, including some of the country's most notorious federal penitentiaries.

"Today I thought that since it's such a lovely summer day we might adjourn to my chateau overlooking the Western Mountain Range, if that meets with your approval, sir," he said, springing up from his chair to greet me.

"Yeah, sure, Jake," I said. "Sure, sure, that would be great!"

I didn't want to give the impression that I was at all surprised by the news that he owns a chateau overlooking the Western Mountain Range.

"Our chariot awaits!" he laughed, throwing his black leather jacket on. "Follow me!"

Just about every person we met in the hallways leading to the elevator turned out to be an ol' buddy of Jake's too, and I felt like I was part of something.

"Hi Jake!" a guy dragging a full trash bag yelled out.

"Pick that thing up and sling it over your shoulder like a man, Mark! You've got to use those muscles, or they'll get soft and they'll be flushing you down the toilet before long!" Jake barked.

VOLUME ONE

So, of course, Mark laughed with delight and, after a little struggle, managed to sling the bag over his shoulder.

"You've got it, man! Go for it!" Jake yelled, pumping his fist into the air.

"He's in my fitness training class," he said as we marched down the hallway. "We meet twice a week for an hour in the rec room. I get them moving around and feeling good about themselves. I've been turning people on to the benefits of fitness training all my life. I started lifting weights when I was a teenager, shortly after I stabbed that guy in the ass. At that point I knew that violence would always be a big part of my life, so I needed to work hard to become as strong as possible. But I don't insist that everyone I train turns into a muscle man like me, and the very last thing I do is encourage them to be violent. I just want them to be in good shape and feel good about themselves. I've managed and owned a number of health clubs here in Portland and all across this great country, and there's been a lot of people over the years who got their lives turned around as a result of the fitness training they got from yours truly.

"That includes women too," he continued as we stood waiting for the elevator. "When I managed the Vic Tanny Health Club in Santa Monica, California, I introduced the idea of inviting women to join us. At that time, it wasn't at all cool for a woman to lift weights, especially in a smelly gym filled with a bunch of sweaty, grunting men. Women had been members of the health clubs, but they were restricted to using electronically powered wooden rollers to keep trim, that sort of thing. But I brought them in and introduced them to weightlifting, and when they discovered that they could do anything a man could do, they stayed and really got into it. Hey, Vic even threatened to fire me for it. At that time women were strictly for adornment, no hard muscles or standing out in any way besides looking pretty, please. No way I was going to go along with that nonsense, though. I'd long promoted vigorous physical exercise, particularly weight-training, as the way to a natural high for *every* body, and I've been delighted to turn people of both genders onto that enlightened notion for many, many years."

When the elevator door opened there was an elderly woman standing there hunched over her walker, looking downcast and bored with it all, but a wide smile spread across her heavily rouged face when Jake immediately launched into full-flirt mode.

"Connie! Connie! Let's go to your place and tear our clothes off and make mad passionate love all afternoon! Then you can make some fried chicken and we'll munch on it with our feet up watching *Smokey and The Bandit* through our toes on that fantastic wide-screen TV of yours!" he exclaimed, like he was so excited by the prospect of it all that he could hardly hold himself back.

"It's a date! It's a date!" she gushed, reaching out and taking his hand and pressing it to her cheek and playfully batting her eyes up at him as we descended to the ground floor, where he theatrically tore himself away from her and said: "Til' later, doll! I can't wait! I can't wait!"

We exited the elevator chuckling, but as we walked across the lobby, a kind of lull came over Jake. He seemed to be wrestling with something, then when we reached the door, he stopped short and looked over at me for a moment without saying anything, then he began to speak in a clear and precise way, as if it was very important to him that I understood exactly what he was saying.

"I've got to make sure we've got something straight between us. There's something that you need to completely understand, and I want to be sure that you do," he said.

Oh, no, here it comes, I thought. It'll be something about what's going to happen to me if I write something that tips the cops off to this or that situation, particularly if the item concerns him or the Hell's Angels, or maybe it'll be about some other kink in all of this that I wasn't at all aware of at the moment.

But, no, it wasn't about that sort of thing at all.

"I'm worried that you might be getting the wrong impression," he began. "What you just witnessed should not lead you to believe that I am as popular around town as I am with the people in this building. Not everyone likes me the way they do. Living in this place means a great deal to me, and I go out of my way to be as friendly and sociable as I can be. Spending long periods of time in one house of incarceration or another, and a good part of that time being spent in solitary confinement, built a great need in me to hunker down somewhere. I feel most secure when I know that I'm going to be in a certain place for a very long time, and this place is the place I want to be at the moment. 'Doing a life sentence in minimum security' is the way I describe it, and it means a great deal to me.

"Okay," he said, stopping and looking straight into my face when we got to the door, "what I'm getting at here is that there's a lot of people out there in the wider world who don't like me very much, and that's putting it mildly. Some of them are going to be pissed off that you're even talking to me. I've broken a lot of heads and some of them haven't healed properly, if you get my drift. And some of my victims who can no longer speak for themselves have families and friends with long memories. I've always lived by one rule, though, and that is I never hurt anyone who doesn't deserve it. I am not a bully. I have only been violent with other violent men. I never pick on anyone weaker than me. In fact, I won't even fight someone who's obviously much weaker than I am. I go out of my way to defend weak individuals from guys who are strong like I am. The only men I want to fight are other men who are as strong as me and like to fight as much as I do. We spot one another right away.

"It's not just the violence I've been involved in that's made me some enemies, though," he continued. "I've done a lot of illegal things over the years, and I'm sure some of my victims still have me very much in mind. I've made it an absolute law all through my life to never steal from the needy, though, and I've made it a habit to steal from the filthy rich whenever the opportunity has presented itself. I'd never steal someone's five-year-old Ford, for instance. I'd be more likely to sell him a late model BMW for about what he'd pay for a new electric lawn mower. That a working class guy is driving a high-end vehicle I stole from some yuppie puke whose father will buy him a better one the next week makes the transaction very satisfying for me. Money has never meant very much to me anyway. I've had a great deal of it at times, but I've always given most of it away to this one and that one and pissed away what was left.

"But, anyway," he said, as I opened the door for us to go out, "like I told you when we met on the sidewalk, there are those who love me, and there are those who hate me, but no one knows the whole story, so that's what we're going to give them – the real truth. I just don't want you to think that I'm expecting you to glorify me, because I know that there's a lot of people who just couldn't stomach that, including me."

We went out the door and walked down the street in silence, headed for the top floor of a nearby parking garage, where his "chariot" turned out to be a very cool black van, which did double service as his "chateau" providing a wonderful view of the Western Mountain Range, which glistened majestically off in the far distance, miles and miles away from Portland, over the tops of trees and church steeples.

"Isn't this grand!" he exclaimed, spreading his arms to take it all in. "I'm absolutely in love with Portland and one of the best things about it is the far-off views you get from spots like this all around the peninsula. As I've mentioned to you before, my ancestors were among the early settlers of the Portland area, so the place is in my blood. I have chromosomal memories of fighting the Indians down by the pond in Deering Oaks, as a matter of fact. Of course, the Indians were absolutely right in every respect to fight for this ground, and I deeply respect them for it, but that wouldn't have interfered with my fighting to the death against them. I'm a born warrior and what warriors do is fight, so that's what I would have done."

Chromosomal memories? I was thinking.

"But onto the business of the day, sir," he resumed. "The last time we spoke, I told you about the stabbing incident that took place in the year 1952, when I was fourteen years of age, and I presume that you would like to pick up from there today and proceed chronologically thereafter, if I am not mistaken."

"Yup," I said, at which point a seagull alighted on

top of the wall at eye level right in front of us and peered through the windshield at Jake. There's no other way to describe the scene.

"Aha!" Jake exclaimed, "an advance scout! Our little discussion has to be temporarily delayed!" he yelled, reaching back behind the driver's seat and lifting out a large trash bag and pulling it into his lap, then jerking his door open and stepping out of the van with it.

"A nice little lady friend of mine who works at Dunkin' Donuts saves these for me to serve to my seagull friends and we're very grateful to her for it!" he boomed as he reached into the bag and brought out what seemed to be an endless supply of little round doughnuts and threw them one at a time high up into the air for the group of seagulls now circling above him. What with the birds' natural airborne predatory skills, and Jake's enthusiastically sailing them very high up into the air, not one of the little doughnuts even came close to hitting the floor of the parking garage.

Watching him throw the doughnuts to the gulls, having a great time making them dive and dart this way and that, all the time yelling loud encouragements and words of praise to each one of them, I chuckled when it occurred to me that many people around town would like to think of themselves as being ol' buddies with Jake Sawyer the way the seagulls on the top of the parking garage are.

When all the doughnuts were gone, he got back in the van and leaned back in the seat contentedly.

"That fellow over there reminds me a lot of myself," he said, pointing to the "advance guard" gull, who was still there on the wall in front of us, stalking imperiously back and forth.

VOLUME ONE

"Seagulls are a majestic animal and I relate very closely to them. They are ambulatory from birth and spend their childhood and adolescence walking around very awkwardly, bumping into things and getting into all kinds of trouble, just like humans do at that stage of their lives. When they finally learn to fly, though, seagulls become the rulers of all they survey, like I did when I became a Hell's Angel. A seagull can hover like a humming bird, dart down out of the sky like a hawk, and soar like an eagle across great distances with the slightest tip of their wing, and that's just the kind of all-powerful and totally in-control feeling I had when I rode with my Hell's Angels brothers.

"Yes sir, if any shit came down, I know that seagull over there walking along the wall would have my back all the way, just like the way it was with me and my Hell's Angels brothers. I can tell just by the way he handles himself that he's filled with integrity and loyalty. They could pull every feather in his friggin' body out and he wouldn't rat on his friends, just like I wouldn't rat on a friend or anyone else, no matter what my captors did to me, or what they offered me. I've proven that time and time again. I did serious time in federal penitentiaries and turned down large cash incentives because I wouldn't come across with certain names, and sometimes I didn't even like the people I was protecting. I just wouldn't snitch on anyone, ever, no matter who they are or what the circumstances. I know this might sound crazy and seriously overblown to you, but I recognize that same kind of character in that bird over there."

The bird might not have known it, but he'd just been paid the highest compliment Jake Sawyer could pay someone.

"Enough with my friends the seagulls, though! Time to continue on with the exciting saga of ol' Jakie boy's life!" he laughed, slapping the palm of his hand down on the dashboard to signal that it was time to get to work.

GRAMMAR SCHOOL

"Okay, man, let's go way back to years before the stabbing, when I was in first grade at Williard School, South Portland. The teacher I remember most from Williard was Mrs. Hatch, my first grade teacher. She was very kind to me. Most of the teachers didn't care for me because I was the class clown, but Mrs. Hatch kind of smiled and went along with my antics. She had her limits, though. She used to make me sit in the corner behind the piano because I wouldn't stop fooling around with Alexandra Reiche, who was my first love. I don't know where she is now, but I've got a feeling that she's had a happy life. I hope so anyway. She was one of those nice girls that you know just can't lose. I'd like to think that she remembers me, but I suppose if she does it's probably from reading about my exploits in the newspaper years later, when my sitting behind the piano at Willard School had progressed to my sitting in solitary confinement at San Quentin and Lewisburg Federal Penitentiary. Well, in case she reads this, I do want her to know that she kept me company in my darkest hours in places like that. You didn't know I was such a romantic, huh?"

"Ah, no, I didn't," I said.

VOLUME ONE

TEEN ANGEL

I asked Jake how the rest of his adolescence went after he stabbed the guy at age fourteen, and he right away launched into a tale that summed it all up very well.

"Oh, I managed to have a fairly normal adolescence," he began, "except for the fact that I always knew that I was capable of ruthlessly attacking someone bigger and stronger than me when it came down to it. That gave me some underlying confidence, so I did a few things my friends might not have done, I guess."

"Such as?" I asked.

"About a year after the stabbing, when I was a sophomore at South Portland High School, I went to downtown Portland to pick up a package at Woolworth's for my mother, and as I went by the pet department I saw a great number of cages filled with birds. I just couldn't stand to see any creature locked in a cage! Those birds were meant to be as free as I was! They had wings to fly but they were spending their lives locked in cages! I just had to do something about it, I just had to, so I went around and opened the doors of all the cages!

"I was amazed that all the birds didn't fly right out. Only a couple did. I guess birds are like people, there's only a few here and there that have the spirit.

"There was no way I was going to let any of those birds stay in their cages after I opened the doors, though, so I broke open a bag of birdseed and scattered it all over the floor, then they all flew out.

"Nobody in the store noticed what was going on for a while, so the birds had time to eat all the seeds they wanted. Then one of the salesclerks noticed what was up and started yelling in a real high shrill voice: 'The birds are out of their cages! The birds are out of their cages!'

"Employees started running from every direction, but what were they supposed to do? Birds don't just sit there and let you grab them. Whenever someone got close to one it would fly up to the ceiling and perch on one of the long florescent lights up there. It was the longest flight they had had in their lifetime, after all, so they needed to rest. Can you imagine being born to fly, and now you've done it for the first time? Pretty soon there were birds sitting on the lights all over the store.

"Think about it now," he went on, "birds are just like you and me. After they eat, what do they do? Yeah. And they did. All over the damn store. That went over real big in the lingerie department. Oh yeah, Woolworth's had a lunch counter at the time too. Of course, I headed for the door when I saw that everyone was making such a big deal out of the situation. I might be a few ounces short of a full gallon, but I'm not completely stupid.

"The whole city was tittering about the incident for weeks. Business was off a little at Woolworth's for a while, until they got the situation under control. People were going there just to see the birds up on the lights, and weren't buying anything. Oh, the public loved it! The store was full of people all day. There weren't as many diners at the lunch counter as usual, though.

"The newspapers ran quite a story about it. They referred to it as a 'prank.' I wasn't too happy about that. I was a liberator, not a damn prankster. I've always hated it when the press got it wrong about some of the things I've done.

"My mother was sitting in the living room reading the newspaper the day after the incident, and I still laugh to myself when I think of her lowering the newspaper and peering at me over the top of her glasses with a little smile, saying: 'Thank you for picking up my package at Woolworth's yesterday, Jonathan.'"

SOUTH PORTLAND HIGH

"When I went to South Portland High it was located in the building that is now Mahoney Middle School, which is named for Daniel F. Mahoney, who was principal of the high school when I went there. Even though Mr. Mahoney had to come down hard on me now and then, I had a great deal of respect for him and I'm very happy that a school got named after him.

"Mr. Mahoney and I got along pretty well, actually. I think he liked that I wasn't a bully like a lot of the other tough guys were. I'd always go up to the unpopular kids who were standing by themselves off to the side and joke around with them, and Mr. Mahoney noticed that. He didn't miss much, and he'd show up in some very unlikely places, too. I respected him because he had a wooden leg but didn't let it slow him down a bit.

"I wasn't much of a student at South Portland High because I spent a lot of time fooling around. My failure to get with the program really grabbed the teachers because I had scored very high on the aptitude test they give you when you start high school. Teachers hate it when you have more ability than they do but don't get with the program.

"The teachers and everybody else put up with a lot from me, though. Even though I was a terrible student and a serious behavior problem, everybody liked me. I pulled a lot of pranks and was always disrupting things, but I never did anything mean to anyone. I don't know exactly where it came from, but I always identified with people who are on the fringes. I went out of my way to ask the unpopular girls to dance, things like that. A lot of the other guys didn't want to be seen on the dance floor with them. Not me. To tell the truth, I actually liked the unpopular girls more than I did the popular ones. They were more real. They cared about you in a way that the pretty popular girls didn't. I'm a hard-ass outlaw to a lot of people, but the ones who really know me know that underneath my tough exterior I'm a real softie."

I'll take that on faith, I said to myself.

"I ended up getting kicked out of South Portland High at the end of my sophomore year. There was this bully that I really didn't like, and one day I threw him down a flight of stairs. Everyone who witnessed it gave a great big cheer, but unfortunately Mr. Mahoney was standing at the bottom of the stairs where the bully landed, and he got knocked on his ass, which dislocated his wooden leg. I felt really shitty about that because, like I said, I liked Mr. Mahoney. I apologized up and down while he was sitting on the floor fixing his leg, but he just couldn't overlook what I'd done. A lot of kids had seen it happen and if he didn't come down hard on me they would've lost respect for him. So I was history.

"When I run into someone today I went to South Portland High with, they always bring up the time I threw that bully down the stairs and he collided with Mr. Mahoney. They laugh like hell about Mr. Mahoney sitting on the floor all flustered, working like mad to readjust his wooden leg, but I didn't think it was funny then, and I don't now.

"You know, most of the people I grew up with in South Portland and went to high school with had no idea who I really was. They didn't get me then, and they don't get me today either. Ah-h-h, ain't that the way it always is with the great ones!"

KENT'S HILL PREP SCHOOL

"Getting kicked out of high school could have been curtains for me, as far as having any kind of life to speak of, but I was from a prominent family, so instead of ending up in a reform school, where I would have formed associations that would have set me up for a life of petty crime and unfulfilled dreams, I was given the option of enrolling at Kent's Hill Preparatory School, which is a prestigious prep school up in Kent's Hill, Maine, about sixty miles north of Portland. A very high percentage of Kent's Hill graduates go on to Ivy League colleges and become movers and shakers in their chosen professions, but at this point I can say in all humility that I am the only one who has risen to the heights of becoming a patch-holding member of the Hell's Angels Motorcycle Club."

"Okay," I said to myself, "Jake Sawyer went to Kent's Hill Prep School. This is definitely not what I had expected."

"I had agreed to go to Kent's Hill because I didn't want to go to reform school," he continued, "but I dreaded living in a dorm with a bunch of yuppie puppies and basically being imprisoned on the grounds of a snooty school up in the boonies. After a while, though, the place grew on me to the point where I absolutely loved it there. The security and predictability of it all was like a salve to my soul.

"I actually felt relaxed for the first time in my life. My home life had been hectic and filled with a great deal of stress. The situation I have described for you with my mother had been going on for years and the anger and resentment I felt towards my father wore very heavily on me, especially after the stabbing, when I knew that my mother respected me more than she respected him. I felt a great deal of anxiety at school as well. I was so much into acting out and being the center of attention that I had a huge reputation to live up to. It was almost as if I would've disappointed people by settling down and becoming a good student. I was in a box that I had put myself into and couldn't get out of, and Kent's Hill proved to be just what I needed at the time. I have always known that I have a guardian angel looking over me and I felt her presence very strongly at that particular time. We will definitely hear more about my guardian angel as we go on, sir, since she has been right there by my side on many, many different occasions."

"She?" I asked.

"Yes!" Jake answered. "I'm aware that most people are assigned a guardian angel of their own gender, but I have been aware from a very early age that my guardian angel is female. Why that is, I don't know, but I do know that I have felt her presence all through my life and that I, without a doubt, would not be here relating these fantastic tales to you had she not been with me at all times."

What interested me was not so much that Jake thinks of his guardian angel as being a female, but

A lively gathering of Kent's Hill students, mid-winter, 1957, with Jake on the far right giving a boost to a buddy while making time with a lovely lass.

that Jake Sawyer would even be talking about having a guardian angel.

"But back to the subject at hand," he began, "I started with a clean slate at Kent's Hill and the expectations were the same for me as they were for everyone else. The ground rules were clear from the very beginning. If I screwed around I would be out on my ass in short order, and I didn't want that. Believe it or not, I pretty much stayed out of major trouble, and even ended up being on the honor roll quite often and graduating in very good standing. I'm also happy to say that I made friends with people at Kent's Hill that I'm still in touch with today."

Okay, a former Hell's Angel and ex-con with a slew of enemies who graduated from a prestigious prep school in very good standing and is still friends with a lot of people he went to school with. The imperious seagull strutting along the top of the wall wasn't the only rare bird on the top floor of the parking garage that day.

"It isn't as if I didn't have a few high adventures at Kent's Hill, though ..."

Aha!

"My roommate, Jack Morse, and I were very close and had a lot in common. We both liked guns, surprise, surprise, and Jack had a black powder pistol that I really wanted. Even then I was very aware of my ancestral heritage, so I knew that my line of Sawyers had fought in the Revolutionary War using black powder pistols, and somehow I had convinced myself that the one Jack owned had been used by my great-great grandfather.

"There wasn't anything I owned that Jack wanted, and he had all the money he needed, so the only thing to do was get a little imaginative. We both got off on adrenalin rushes and liked to dare each other to do crazy and dangerous things, so I made Jack an offer I knew he wouldn't refuse.

"The central building on the Kent's Hill campus is Bearce Hall, which is a towering, four-story-high 1850s brick building with the American and State of Maine flags flying from the dome. There's an apple orchard across the way from Bearce Hall a little bit, and I got Jack to agree that if I went over and got an apple and climbed up the side of Bearce Hall and stuck it on the top of the flagpole, he'd give me the pistol. Jack was sure I couldn't do it, but he knew that I would just about die trying, so he was looking forward to the show.

"We had to get up at five in the morning to pull it off, because if anyone saw us, we were done for. Preppies like to tattle. The deal was that I had to climb up the side of the building, right from the bottom, without using drainpipes or anything else except toeholds I could get in the brick. It was hard as hell at first, and I kept falling off, but I really wanted my great-great-grandfather's pistol, so I kept at it. Fortunately, the brick-work on a hundred year old building is pretty rough and there's a lot of crevices, so eventually I began to make some headway, and after about an hour and a half of intense effort, knowing that I might fall off and break every bone in my friggin' body at any time, I made it to the top of the roof.

"Then I had to shinny up the flagpole. I didn't think that was going to be a problem at all, but I found out that flagpoles are soaking wet early in the morning, and I kept slipping down. So, I had to take off my shirt and wipe off the pole as I went along. The hardest part was when I got closer to the top, because the shirt was

Bearce Hall, Kent's Hill Prep School

soaking wet by that time. I could have grabbed onto the American flag, it would have really helped, but I'm too much of a patriot to do that. Jack was laughing his ass off down on the ground and yelling up that I'd never make it. When he started singing 'God Bless America,' though, I got to laughing so hard I almost fell off the friggin' pole.

"Finally, I made it to the top of the pole without grabbing onto the flag! What a feeling it was when I plunked that apple down onto the top of that flagpole! Whump!"

I looked up from my scribbling to see his re-enactment of that crowning moment, and I wasn't disappointed.

"Whump!" he yelled again, arching his arm up and plunking that apple down on that flagpole forever.

"Unfortunately, all didn't end well. Going back down the building, which should have been the easy part, I got a little careless and fell from the second floor to the ground and broke my ankle.

"What really hurt about that, though, was that the cast I had to wear on my ankle became first-hand evidence of my wrongdoing. The whole school was buzzing about how that apple could have gotten up there, and as soon as I showed up with that friggin' cast on my ankle everyone knew for sure what was up. I didn't mind about them knowing that I had put the apple on top of the flagpole, of course, but I wasn't crazy about the girls knowing that I fell off the building on the way down. Made me look like a klutz, you know?

"Oh well, I did come into possession of that black powder pistol, and that's all that mattered, I guess."

Somehow I knew what I'd be thinking of the next time I saw the American flag flying on a high building.

JAKE

*Jake perched on the fire escape of his dormitory,
proudly displaying the cast on his right leg he
acquired after falling off the side of Bearce Hall.*

Jake, wearing number 13, played Center on the team.

"For some reason," Jake says, chuckling, "my basketball coach got a big kick out of me wearing number 13. He said it somehow looked just right on me."

JAKE

A BLEMISHED SPORTS CAREER

"Yes, all in all, Kent's Hill was good to me," Jake went on. "As well as being a good student and staying out of serious trouble, I was also very active in sports there. I was on three varsity sports teams, in fact: basketball, football and track. I'd been lifting weights very seriously for a few years by that time, and was a good deal stronger than my peers were, so that definitely worked to my advantage.

"My biggest memory of my football career was being kicked out of the Fryeburg Academy game. I wasn't being a very good sport, I guess. I thought the idea was to put opposition players out of commission, and that's what I always tried to do, any way I could. I guess I got a little too much into it or something, though, because I ended up flattening two opposing players. 'Unnecessary Roughness,' they called it. The officials kicked me out of the game and the coach made me go sit on the bus, which really fried my ass because I had my eye on one of the Fryeburg Academy cheerleaders and when she saw me sitting on the bus it kind of tarnished my image with her. Evidently she wasn't completely turned off, though. She and I came across one another at the supermarket not long ago and we recognized each other right away, and before long our mutual pent-up desires got satisfied big time. Hey, what's a few streaks of gray hair mean when it comes to reuniting with an old friend?

"I had quite a career at Kent's Hill in basketball, too. I was six-two and aggressive as hell, so the coach made me the Center on the team. I'd spend the whole game basically beating people up, like I did in football. There was this one guy from Windham High who was bigger and stronger than me, though, and he kept bullying me the whole game. You know how I hate bullies, so I became quite pissed off with him, as you might suppose I would. At one point I punched him in the nose so hard blood gushed all over the court. I happened to see the guy on the street a number of years later and noticed that his nose was quite flat. I suppose I should have felt bad about it but, you know, I hate bullies so much that I didn't feel bad at all.

"I had to go to the headmaster's office after the incident, but that didn't amount to much. The headmaster's name was William Dunn, and he and I got along real well, just like I got along with Mr. Mahoney real well at South Portland High. They were both rugged, all-around regular guys and we could relate to each other. Mr. Dunn had been a hockey player in college, and when he told me I shouldn't play so rough it was all he could do to keep from cracking up.

Practicing the high-jump at the state
championship track meet.

JAKE

Jake says he was too light to be more than an average shot-putter, but he loved competing in the event.

"My athletic career at Kent's Hill was quite well rounded, actually. I was also on the track team and ran the one-hundred-yard dash in 10.1 seconds, which was quite fast. I also broad jumped a little over nineteen feet. Track was my best sport, performance-wise, no question. I relied on brute strength and intimidation in basketball and football, but track required focus and discipline, and I found that it was good for my mental development.

"There is more of a spotlight on your individual performance in track than there is in other sports, so it had that appeal too. One might say that there were often ulterior motives to my participation in athletics, in general, but track in particular. I still have a picture of myself and a little brunette I was dating at the time posing together after I won a race or something. For some reason or other, she was really turned on by track stars. She was definitely a hot little piece and I scratched a lot of itches with her, but I dumped her for a leggy blond shortly after the picture was taken.

"The brunette was there at our fiftieth Kent's Hill class reunion with her husband. He's a mucky muck, wears a bow tie and white and black patent leather shoes. It's his trademark or something. Because of him, of course, she couldn't acknowledge me in any way, but I got a nice little look from her, which told me she hadn't forgotten a thing. I knew that for friggin' sure. I really enjoyed that and I thought about it all the time I was roaring down the highway on my Harley. I didn't get recognized from the podium or anything, like a lot of the others did, but I was happy I went to the reunion anyway, mostly because of her and the happy memories she brought back. She might have been sitting in the passenger seat of a new Mercedes Benz on the ride home, but I knew she was smiling to herself thinking about me grinning over at her, revvin' up my bike, being the bad boy she knew so many years ago and still sorta loved.

"Hey, a man's gotta have his beliefs!"

THREE

Now that I had been to Jake's apartment and found out that it wasn't anything like the outlaw-biker crash pad I thought it would be, I called him and suggested that we have our next talk there. Sitting in his cool black van on top of the parking garage getting to know his seagull buddies was fun, but I enjoyed meeting in his apartment. Jake's the perfect host, like he told me his mother was, and the pictures and memorabilia of his life all over the walls provided the ideal background for our talks. When I arrived and complimented him on his living accommodations, I could see that he was pleased to hear it.

"I have been waiting for just this kind of living situation for a long, long time," he said. "Spacious rooms, and a lot of wall space that I can fill any way I want to. As you know, I have spent a number of years of my life incarcerated in one lock-up or another, and wall space that you can do what you want with is one of the privileges you lose when the cell door clangs shut behind you. There are also extremely strict rules for what could be put on the walls, which is often just a calendar to scratch off the days, and maybe a picture of your mother or some other woman, and one of your kids, if you have any. Your kids grow up and you'd still have that picture of them when they were five years old up on the wall. There's a glimpse of prison life for you. Great, huh?"

"It's beyond anything I can imagine, Jake," I said.

"Right! At least you know it! A lot of people think they know what it's like, but they don't know shit! There's no damn windows in some prison cells!" he roared, striding over to his living room window and spreading his arms to take in the beauty of Casco Bay. "Ahhh ... ain't this grand!"

He insisted that I come over and look through the telescope he has mounted on a tripod in front of the window facing the harbor. Wow! I could see the people on the deck of a Casco Bay Lines ferry, and I could read the names of the sailboats tied up at the marina way across the bay over in South Portland!

"Sometimes I sit here all alone smiling to myself as I look across Portland Harbor over at the Coast Guard base in South Portland that I stole a million dollars in marijuana from," he chuckled. "You must have heard about that one, right?"

I told him that I sure as hell remembered the incident, what local wouldn't? Stealing that much seized pot from under the noses of the feds doesn't happen every day, but I told him that it was a story for another day, and because he was always willing to cooperate with anything he saw as leading to the successful completion of the book, he immediately nodded his head in agreement.

"So let's get to it, Jake," I said. "The last time we talked you had graduated from Kent's Hill, so where did you go from there?"

NORWICH UNIVERSITY

"After Kent's Hill I enrolled at Norwich University, which is the oldest private military school in America, and is considered to be on a par with West Point. I got into Norwich because of my good record at Kent's Hill, both as a student and as a standout in three varsity sports. The big thing in my favor, though, was the good recommendation I got from the headmaster. As I've said, Mr. Dunn was a rough and tumble man's man like me, and he was convinced that I would make an an outstanding military officer. That, of course, pleased me very much because I had known from a very early age that I had an almost uncanny ability to exert my influence over other men. I had also known from an early age that it was my destiny to someday engage in mortal combat with the enemies of America, so I saw going to a military academy as a step on the way to fulfilling my destiny.

Officer material all the way...

"Norwich wasn't for me, though. They soon found out that I'm a natural born leader of men, and obviously that was pretty important, but to be an officer you also have to set a good example for the enlisted men, which means having a spotless disciplinary record. Yeah, right. I, without question, might still hold the Norwich record for most demerits for misbehavior of one kind or another for the one and a half year time period that I was there. I maybe even got enough demerits to set the four year record, who knows? At any rate, it's damn cold in the winter in Vermont, and I did a whole lot of marching around the parade field with my rifle on my shoulder as punishment. I would laugh at it, though, just like I always have with everything I've done, and they didn't like my attitude at all. I don't know how I lasted there as long as I did. I was always marching up and down the parade field when everybody else had free time, like afternoons after classes and most weekends, and that was a real pain in the ass.

"I did get to be the go-to guy for how to survive those hours working off your demerits in the Vermont cold on the parade field, though. I'd smuggle a bottle of booze into the dormitory and carry it under my jacket out onto the parade field, then when I'd get a break from marching to use the latrine, I'd take a few hits and stash the bottle in the tank of the toilet. All my friends knew, of course, that they could always count on finding a bottle of booze in the toilet tank when they were marching off their demerits. When they were back out on the field and were inebriated as hell and numb to it all, they'd be smiling about what a great guy that Jake Sawyer was. I was just trying to keep us warm on very cold days.

"Hey, that's not much of a legacy, I guess, but I

know without a doubt that when certain retired Generals gather at their Norwich class reunion today, one of the things they chuckle together about is getting high on the booze ol' Jakie boy left in the toilet tank in the latrine just off the parade field. They've probably got a plaque on the latrine by this time with my name on it!"

"Yeah!" I agreed, "you're in the annals of military history!"

"Be careful how you pronounce that!" he laughed.

"There was just too much regimentation at Norwich, though," he continued, still chuckling to himself. "That's like saying there was too much singing in voice training school, I guess, but whatever. I was on the drill team and I liked that, so maybe I took to the regimentation to some degree, after all. To stay on the drill team, you had to stay in perfect lock-step, and you had to have all the precision movements down so that nothing you did stood out from what the others were doing. The most dreaded thing they could label you as was what they called an 'individual.' Imagine *me* in a situation like that. But I actually did well as a member of the drill team. I guess underneath all my rebelliousness I liked the comfort and security of military regimen. Haven't quite figured that one out myself, but there it is. I was a cracker-jack, right by the book, fully compliant member of the drill team. That was my only connection to greatness at Norwich, though, and early in the second semester of my sophomore year, I walked out the front door in my civilian clothes, smiling all the way."

THE U.S. ARMY

"After Norwich, in the Spring of 1959, when I was twenty-one," Jake continued, "I really didn't have much desire to pursue an academic education, so I didn't give any thought to transferring to another college. I did know, however, that I had always thrived in the company of men and was always respected among them – and I also knew that it was my destiny as a loyal American to engage in combat with the enemies of America – so I decided to join the Army.

"I was sent to Ft. Dix, New Jersey, for Basic Training, but that didn't amount to much after what I'd been through at Norwich, so I got through it without too much of a problem. Hey, I still feel a kind of bond between me and the guys I want through Basic Training with, you know what I mean?"

"Yeah, I do," I said, "yeah, I do."

"Once I was a graduate of Army Basic Training and ready for combat the Army, of course, sent me to Ft.

Gordon, Georgia, to attend Signal Training school. There wasn't a war going on at the time, you see, and they took the occasion to cross-train me. Needless to say, I was extremely bored at Ft. Gordon and was desperate for any kind of stimulation I could find.

"When I had any free time at Ft. Gordon," he continued, "I would take the bus into Augusta, which is a fairly large city and offers a wide range of attractions for a young soldier, many of which I availed myself of. My favorite haunt got to be a bar named *The Nineteenth Hole*, on Main Street, where I became acquainted with a blonde waitress who took me home with her pretty regularly and gave me something to think about on my bus ride back to Ft. Gordon the next morning.

"My tenure at Ft. Gordon was cut short when I intentionally flunked out of Signal School. That has to be an all-time low for anybody, flunking out of Signal School, but if I hadn't gotten out of there I might have died from boredom, which would have been an unfortunate epitaph, after all I'd been through, and in light of the scintillating future that lay before me.

"Next stop, Sandy Hook, New Jersey, to attend Radar School. My Commanding Officer thought it would be just the thing for me, because I had done well in science and math at both Kent's Hill and Norwich, but I found Radar School to be extremely boring too, not to mention that I had no desire to confront the enemies of America armed only with technological expertise. I was born to engage in mortal hand-to-hand combat with my adversaries, not track them across a radar screen and push a button and blow them to smithereens. Somehow that lacks the man-to-man contact I've always preferred.

"Things were humming along very well for me

during that time, but extenuating circumstances a-rose, as they always have throughout my life. Out of nowhere, through no fault of my own, certainly, I got involved in a barroom brawl in downtown Sandy Hook and the New Jersey police had to be called in to break it up. For some reason, I was one of the ones arrested, even though I was getting the crap beat out of me right before they put the cuffs on me. They were told by the owner that it might be advisable, I guess, since I was the one responsible for keeping the fight going. I wasn't even involved in the issue that ignited the fireworks, actually, and never did find out what the fight was all about. I just jumped in because I love to fight. I am sure I pummeled combatants from both sides. Maybe I ended up giving one side or the other the edge, I didn't know or care.

"The guy who ended up beating the shit out of me had stayed out of the fight, but after it started to calm down I looked over at him and called him a fucking chicken, and that was it. Right away he got a fire in his eye that told me it was going to be one helluva fight. He was on me from the gitgo, and beat me to the floor before I knew what was happening. I was probably three inches taller than him, about thirty pounds heavier, and about twice as strong, but he was madder than I was. I was in it for recreation, just because I love fighting, but he was in it as a matter of principle. Your motivation makes all the difference in a fight, you know.

"It wasn't the first fight I'd ever lost, and it wasn't going to be the last one either. I've lost fights, sure, but I've never backed down from one. Any man who likes to fight and says he's never lost one is a lying fuck. If you get into a lot of fights, you're going to lose one now and then. What's different about degenerate fools like me is that getting beat doesn't deter us to any degree at all. After we lose, we look for somebody bigger than we are to fight the next time, as a way to get our confidence back. When fighting is in your genes, you keep fighting, no matter what.

"Anyway, my Company Commander at Radar School wasn't too impressed with my extracurricular activities, and I knew I was looking at spending some time in an Army jail. That didn't sound like much fun, actually, but my Company Commander took me aside and said he'd forget all about the incident if I would agree to leave Radar School and volunteer for paratrooper training. Anything was better than doing six months in the stockade at Ft. Dix, New Jersey, which was not very far away, and I had always been attracted to extremes anyway, so here we go. I jumped into my two-toned blue, two door 1954 Oldsmobile 98 the very next morning and headed west to Ft. Campbell, Kentucky, all hopped up about jumping out of airplanes and landing behind enemy lines to engage the enemies of America in mortal hand-to-hand combat."

U.S. ARMY AIRBORNE PARATROOPER

"As I hopped into my very smooth running Oldsmobile and headed out from Sandy Hook, New Jersey, to Ft. Campbell, Kentucky, I was all excited to find out what this grand new adventure was going to be all about. When I arrived at the front gate of Ft. Campbell and saw a display of two badly damaged cars, with a number of polished jump boots lined up in front of them, I got an immediate impression of the intensity

Sign over the entrance of the Ft. Campbell, Kentucky paratrooper jump school.

of the training I was about to experience. There were a couple of used car dealerships across the state highway from Ft. Campbell that sold used vehicles for $100 down and $50 a month thereafter, so it was an easy matter for a trainee on leave to acquire a vehicle, and with the pent-up anxiety inside trainees, accidents were common. Uncle Sugar obviously wanted to ensure that after all the time and expense of training young men to be dropped into hazardous areas to do battle with the enemies of America, that those young men didn't end their young lives on the highway between Ft. Campbell and Nashville, Tennessee, where they went to party down very hard at numerous honky-tonk bars located there.

"Paratrooper training at Fort Campbell was on a whole other planet than either Norwich or Basic Training at Ft. Dix had been. They pushed us so hard at Ft. Campbell that we all thought we were going to friggin' die. I'd been lifting weights very regularly for about ten years by then, so I was pretty strong, but they worked me hard, no question. No matter who you are, or how strong you are, they broke you down and built you back up.

"They had a sign up over the front entrance to the jump school at Ft. Campbell that said, 'Rendezvous with Destiny,' but I didn't find the experience to be all that romantic. I was there in the middle of August, and Kentucky gets pretty hot in the summer, at least for a New England boy. Running ten miles or more at double-time in the ninety-plus Kentucky heat was an interesting contrast to marching on the Norwich parade grounds in Vermont in the sub-zero dead of winter. Neither one was a lot of fun, but I think I'd choose feeling like you're going to freeze to death over being fried to a crisp. At least when you're freezing to death after a while you don't feel anything.

"Getting to be a United States Airborne Paratrooper was tough, no question. The training cadre, who are called 'Black Hats' worked us hard and tried to break our spirit every way they could. They knew each one of us was there because we wanted to be counted among the elite of the elite, and their job was to make sure that not one of us made it across the finish line who wasn't exactly that.

"Paratrooper training is broken up into three gruesome weeks: Ground Week, Tower Week, and Jump Week. Ground Week is filled with brutal harassment by the Black Hats, running for hours in the scorching hot sun with full backpacks, and culminates in practicing and perfecting the Parachute Landing Fall, commonly known as the PLF, whereby it is drilled into the trainees consciousness that following the Seven Points of Contact procedure to the slightest detail will always result in a safe landing. Ground Week culminates in practice landings from the Lateral Drift Assembly, which features a zip line coming down from a thirty-four-foot tower, and if a trainee hadn't completely mastered the Seven Points of Contact procedure, he was gone.

"The wash-out rate in paratrooper training is very high, and the majority of the quitters did so by the end of Ground Week. There was an embankment off to the side that had a huge sign on it saying 'Quitters Row' and the Black Hats were constantly reminding us that all we had to do is walk over there and step up onto that embankment and our agony would be over. Quitters had to stand on the embankment for three hours at parade rest, just so everybody present would remember you forever as a quitter. I would have died before I joined Quitter's Row, of course, but sometimes

JAKE

I thought that death might actually be my only way out of the shit I was going through.

"The Black Hats were right on me from the very beginning because I had made the biggest mistake a trainee could make: I did something to draw attention to myself. Standing out in the group was to be avoided at all costs, but that's exactly what I did. There was this one guy who was always getting picked on by the other trainees because he was kind of small. I don't know why he was even there. I think he must have had some kind of a fantasy about jumping out of airplanes, or maybe he was trying to become a man in his father's eyes. We had bare-your-soul sessions as part of the program, and a very high number of men said that gaining their father's approval was their main motivation for wanting to be a paratrooper. It wasn't mine, of course. I was after impressing myself, and staying out of the Ft. Dix stockade, and that was it. I had made a decision early-on to always go for the gusto under any and all circumstance, and in this instance that meant becoming a United States Army Airborne Paratrooper.

"So, when I saw one of my fellow trainees giving the guy a hard time to impress the Black Hats, I went over and punched the bully's lights out. That felt very satisfying, and it endeared me to the other trainees, but the Black Hats immediately branded me as a grandstander and a 'fucking individual,' and what you have to understand here is that an 'individual' is the worst thing a trainee could be called. When you fall from the sky and land in enemy territory you are often entirely dependent upon your fellow paratrooper for your survival, and being an individual is not what that's all about."

VOLUME ONE

THE SWING LANDING TRAINER

"The Swing Landing Trainer, or SLT, is commonly refer-red to as either 'The Devil's Torture Device' or 'The Nut Cracker,' and its main purpose is to train people in 'mass exit procedure,' which has to do with learning how to jump out of an airplane as part of a line of men who are following the same precise procedure you all have been taught. The line of men shuffles up onto the platform of the SLT, each of you hooks up to an overhead cable, then jumps off the platform into a sand pit. You must, of course, land exactly according to the Seven Points of Contact, then immediately jump up and get out of the pit, because in combat the enemies of America do not allow you to do so in a leis-urely manner.

"Well, what happened on one occasion was that a friend of mine didn't get up fast enough to please the Black Hats and the big, tough trainee they had stationed in the landing pit to yank slow-moving people up was unnecessarily rough with him. He hoisted him up by the waist and shook him around, you know, to get everybody laughing, which pissed me off big time. So when it was my turn to fall into the pit I intentionally took my time getting up, and when the fucking bully mucked onto me to yank me up I gave him an elbow in the face. That went over very well with my fellow trainees, but the Black Hats were livid as hell at me, and for punishment I had to 'buck the line,' which meant that I didn't get to go to the end of the line to wait my turn to get onto the SLT again, the way the other trainees did. I had to go right to the front of the line, which means I didn't get a chance to rest and recover. Man, we're talking Kentucky in August. I've never been so hot and completely exhausted in my life. Hey, it was worth it, though. My fellow trainees saw that I'd always have their backs no matter what, and the Black Hats saw the same thing, which is what they look for in a paratrooper, even though that's the last thing they were ever going to let me know at the time.

"The third week, Jump Week, is, as you might surmise, when we got to actually jump out of one of Uncle Sugar's airplanes. In order to become a United States Army paratrooper, one has to have made five successful jumps from an airplane, and I did so, but my next two jumps almost did me in. The first three jumps were what are called 'Hollywood jumps' because the soldier isn't carrying extra equipment but numbers four and five are made carrying a full load of equipment, which makes hitting the ground that much harder.

"After becoming a paratrooper, my next jump took place at Ft. Bragg, North Carolina, where I took part in a ten-thousand-man jump that might still be a record for the most people to jump out of a squadron of airplanes at one time, as far as I know. It was a fantastic sight to behold! Never had the sky been so filled with airborne defenders of America!

"There was a very high wind that day, though, and I hit the ground so hard I couldn't get up. My right leg felt like it was paralyzed. To make matters worse, because of the wind my chute stayed open and pulled me along the ground no matter how hard I tried to pull it towards me. When the wind calmed down a bit, I was finally able to pull the chute towards me, but I still couldn't get up.

"They came and got me in an ambulance and brought me to the base hospital, where I counted eighteen other men laying on stretchers in the same condition I was in. I was worried for us all, of course, but we were assured by the attending medical people that after a shot of whatever muscle relaxant they gave us, we'd all soon be good to go, and we were, after about an hour. Damn, I don't know what that stuff was, but it did the trick. All I know is that I felt damn grateful and relieved when I was able to swing my leg out of that bed and stand up and get dressed by myself."

Jonathan "Jake" Sawyer

Jake before his first jump.

JAKE

LIFE AS A PARATROOPER

"I ended up making a total of twenty-two jumps out of Uncle Sugar's airplanes, and I will assure you that jumping out of an airplane into the clear blue sky is an absolutely glorious experience. The only other time my spirit has been set so free is a few years later when I rode with my Hell's Angels brothers doing 90 miles an hour weaving in and out of traffic on a crowded California freeway.

"I loved jumping out of airplanes. They assigned you a jump manifest you weren't supposed to deviate from that called for you to make one jump a month, but I've always been very good at manipulating other males to do my bidding, so I managed to jump a total of twenty-two times in one three month period.

"What you have to understand here is that as a paratrooper I was much admired around the base. Most of the other paratroopers got sent to Army bases around the world, so most of the GI's stationed there at Ft. Campbell were clerks and such, you know, non-combatants, and here I was trained to jump into the sky and land in hostile territory to engage in mortal hand-to-hand combat with enemies of America."

"Jake, I, ah … "

"Anyway," he continued, unaware that I had started to say something, "because there were no enemies of America that needed tending to at the time, I had to hang around Ft. Campbell after I had earned my silver wings. Because of my status as a paratrooper, though, I was able to get away with a wide variety of mischief.

"Oh, I must tell you about my nighttime activities on the parade field. A lot of the other GIs at Ft. Campbell were female, you see, and they tended to start creaming in their green Army fatigues whenever they happened to be in the presence of a paratrooper. I'd simply invite them for an evening stroll, we'd somehow end up out in the middle of the parade field, and all sorts of wanton acts occurred between us at that point. Why the parade field, I don't know, but there you go. Ain't life grand?"

A KENTUCKY RUM-RUNNER

"I was stationed at Ft. Campbell for almost a year after my paratrooper training," Jake went on, "during which time I frequented some of the local bars in my off-time, as was my custom wherever I was stationed in the Army. I made friends with a bunch of good ol' boys downtown, and we had some high ol' times together, that I can tell you. Getting drunk on moonshine, fighting anybody anytime, and chasing women full time. Everybody kidded me about my Northern accent, but they liked me. They had no idea they made Yankees like me, they said.

"Things got really interesting, though, when I started running moonshine for them in my merry Oldsmobile. I installed Monroe Load Levelers so I could carry about 200 gallons of the stuff in my trunk and the ass-end wouldn't sag and draw the attention of the police. I made some good money running moonshine and had a helluva good time at it. One of the main joys of it all was that the women in the area liked moonshiners very much because they were a gutsy adventuresome bunch and always had a lot of dough in their pockets. You've heard about what Kentucky women are like, haven't you?"

JAKE

"Yes!" I exclaimed.

"I ran moonshine for three months or so on a fairly regular basis," he continued, after a kind of a quizzical look over at me, "which is what my suppliers called 'a good run.' Usually new drivers didn't last quite that long, especially if they weren't from the area, mostly because of the law-enforcement factor. The police might not catch up to you after they spotted you speed-ing down the highway with a tell-tale lowered rear-end, but they usually got a good look at you, and some early evening when you were sitting at a rest-aurant counter with your girlfriend, they'll come up behind you, pull your arms back, and slap hand-cuffs on your wrists.

Jake's '54 Olds, complete with the Monroe Load Levelers he installed so that the rear-end wouldn't sink when the trunk was filled with moonshine.

"I didn't play the game the way those good ol' boys played it, though. I never drove at a high speed and there was nothing about me or my car that looked suspicious. The kicker was that I kept my paratrooper uniform hanging in one of the back side-windows, where it was visible to any and all officers of the law. Paratroopers were so well respected by the police that it never even occurred to them that one of us would be a moonshine runner in his spare time. I'd often cruise by police speed traps where they'd give me one of those quick buddy-buddy nods, or maybe even a friendly little wave.

"It had to end, though, and it did. Another paratrooper found out that I was doing it and tried to do it himself and got busted. What gave him away was the guilty way he acted. He stopped for gas and made a point of waving at some state police that pulled up across the parking lot from him before they waved at him, which was a serious mistake, of course. He even removed his uniform from the rear window and dusted it off while they were looking, just so he'd be sure they saw it. Oh, what an idiot. Just the kind of thing police look for. As soon as they saw him dusting off his uniform and smiling over at them, their suspicions about the lowered back-end of his car were confirmed and he was history. I'd had a lot of experience at working the other side of the fence, so I knew how to go about my business, but he didn't. Needless to say, after the other paratrooper got busted, my paratrooper cover was blown, and that was it for my rum running days.

"Running moonshine was great while it lasted, though. I remember being in hog heaven, tooling down those Kentucky back roads with the radio blaring and 200 gallons of high-quality moonshine hooch in the trunk singing my head off!

JAKE

"*Thunder was his engine, and white lighting was his load ...*" he crooned.

"Robert Mitchum, 'The Ballad of Thunder Road,' recorded in 1958!" I exclaimed.

"That's right!" he yelled back, thrusting his fist into the air.

"The United States Army and I parted company in 1961," he continued, still chuckling, "and I have to say I look back on those days with great fondness. I never did get to engage directly with the enemies of America in hand to hand mortal combat, but I was ready and willing and that counts for a lot, right?"

"Yes, Jake, it does. By the way," I said, with a little hesitation, picking up on what I'd started to tell him before, and not quite sure how he'd react, "I was stationed in Kentucky myself when I was in the Army, about five or six years after you were. I was at Ft. Knox, as a non-combatant Specialist 5 Food Inspector, and I made some food inspection trips to Ft. Campbell."

At this, Jake immediately jumped up from his chair and came across the room with his hand extended, whereupon I stood up, looked him straight in the eye, shook hands with him, and we both yelled: "Go Army! Thank you for your service!"

FOUR

Jake's always spit-and-polish ready and raring to go when I arrive at his place, so I learned that I needed to have my notebook open and pen at the ready from the moment I rapped on the door to announce my arrival.

"Welcome to minimal security, unit zero, my friend! Let's get on with the show!"

"Alright, Jake," I said, hastening to comply. "The last time we spoke we got you out of Uncle Sugar's peacetime Army after two years of fun and adventure. So, what did you do after you were let loose out into the free world as a wild and wholly honorably-discharged U.S. Army paratrooper?"

GENERAL MOTORS DISTRICT SALES MANAGER

"After the Army I scurried back to good ol' Maine, of course," he began, settling back in his chair. "As much as I've been around the country and had a great time everywhere I've been, Maine will always be my home.

"Now the question was what to do with myself, though. My mother said it was time for me to settle down and get a job that would set me up for life, and I knew she was right, so I applied for some pretty good positions and ended up having some attractive options. I had a very good educational background at that point, what with Kent's Hill, Norwich, and the various Army schools I had attended. I was also an honorably discharged U. S. Army paratrooper, and that looked real good at a time when people were starting to avoid their military obligation.

JAKE

"That all looked real good to the job recruiters, but the main thing I had going for me was my ability to influence other men. Add to that that one of my greatest passions in life had always been any and all types of vehicles, so lo and behold, I aced a series of interviews with General Motors and ended up being hired as the company's district sales manager for central Maine. They told me that I was the youngest district sales manager in the country, and that they hired me because they wanted someone with a lot of energy and charisma, someone who could light a fire under the sales crews across the state.

"Ah! I knew I was the man they were looking for all the way! There I was, ready to take on the world, beaming with health and full of confidence, wearing a snappy business suit, carrying a nice leather briefcase my mother bought me, just eager to get on with my chosen career, driving a brand new Chevy, and very happy about the expense account I would be receiving!

"I ended up living in Rumford, a small mill town about one hundred miles northwest of Portland, and just about in the center of my sales district. I got along pretty well with the locals up there because I genuinely felt at ease in their company. They were strictly working class, no pretensions. Usually the employees of the new car dealerships dreaded seeing someone representing the home office come through the door, but once they found out that I was on their side against the hotshots in Detroit, everything was golden. I'd stand in the middle of the showroom talking about this and that Kent's Hill basketball game where I knocked out a couple of the opposing players or something, that kind of thing. They'd get all excited. High school basketball and drunken brawls out in the parking lot of the local diner is about all they've got up there in the winter for excitement. Headquarters was pleased when they got wind of my popularity with what they called 'the boots on the ground people' because they were having some difficulties understanding the Maine character and I seemed to understand it very well. Most important, of course, was that, due to improved morale, new car sales were up. I'd praise hell out of the salespeople when they moved the merchandise out the door, and we'd end up going out on the town to spend their commission checks, thereby bonding us even more.

"The home office in Detroit liked me because not only was I good for morale, I also had a great capacity for detail, which is sometimes hard to find in outgoing socially confident people like me. My military munitions courses at Norwich taught me how to memorize sets of facts and figures and connect them to one another, and my paratrooper training gave me the focus and discipline to sit down and actually do it. I could spout details about every make and model of not only GM vehicles, but also of every make and model of every GM competitor, and I filled my salespeople's heads with endless horseshit about what's good about our vehicles and bad about those of our competitors, to the point where I had them convinced that a customer would have to be an absolute fool not to purchase a GM vehicle.

"Everything was going so well that after I'd been district manager for a year or so, General Motors decided to have the annual East Coast sales conference in Rumford, with me as the host. That was a definite feather in my cap, as the event was attended not only by dealership managers up and down the East Coast, but also by a number of high-up execs from the home office in Detroit. The scuttlebutt was that it wouldn't be long before I was sales manager for the entire State of Maine, then maybe for the Northeast district of the country, and so on up, until the day when I would be a top Detroit muck-a-muck making an obscene fortune selling GM vehicles to deserving Americans all across this great country."

THE COUNTY FAIR

"Oh, but circumstances beyond my control intervened once again in my life! I don't know how I've put up with it all!"

I laughed out loud at that one, which greatly amused Jake.

"One of the functions of the host of the conference was to entertain the group in their free time, and that turned out to be my dead-man's curve, so to speak.

"I took the whole group to the Farmington Fair one night, figuring that that would give them a taste of real Maine life and help with their understanding of the native character. They were used to sitting in dark lounges getting slowly stoned on martinis and trying to look up waitresses' dresses at these sales conferences, so going to a county fair up in Maine would be a nice twist, they all said.

"We had a great time at the fair, too. I introduced them to fried dough, harness racing, and, of course, we went to the strip show. They had never seen anything like that. Anybody who'd ever been to a strip show at a Maine county fair in those days knew that you couldn't see a better strip show anywhere. I suppose that was because the fair came to town and stayed for only a relatively short time, so the authorities didn't pay as much attention to what went on there as they did to what happened at local bars and such.

"That sort of thing doesn't go on today, of course!" he yelled, "'Feminist America' is a drag! Back then men were men and women were glad of it!

"Anyway," he said, after he'd cooled down a bit, "things got really raw. The GM execs got into it, big time. They couldn't believe what they were seeing. The strippers got right down to it right away. There was no wasting time dancing around and teasing for these girls. They came out onto the stage wearing just a long veil and panties, sashayed around a bit, dropped the veil, and stood at the front edge of the stage gyrating and inviting the boys to come up and put bills down their panties. Of course, when the local guys started yelling for them to take the panties off, the girls would tell them that wasn't going to happen until there were enough bills stuffed in them. Smart girls. They knew what they were doing, and they knew how to go about it. I had some fairly extensive experience in the sex trade years later and found that women in that line of work are some of the best and brightest people around.

"Oh my fucking word! Those GM boys didn't quite believe that the strippers would really take their panties off if they got stuffed with enough money, and when the magic moment came those guys went absolutely ballistic!

"'Welcome to Maine!' I yelled.

"They'd never seen that happen at any of the strip clubs they'd been to anywhere else. Where those guys came from, the girls just danced around the stage a little bit in short-shorts and threw winks around the room here and there, I guess. These girls didn't just remove their panties, though. After that came the feelie-feelie part of the show. When my execs saw the locals going up to the edge of the stage and shoving money in the girls' hands and running their hands up their legs a little, they immediately shook their heads, like 'I'd never do that, I'd never do that', but after a few small plastic cups of beer they were falling over themselves to get in line, money in hand.

"There was this one girl who was the most beautiful stripper I've ever seen. Flowing red hair down to her ass, big luscious blue eyes, and an kind of coy, very feminine look about her. She and I got into an eye thing right from the start. Just one of those things that sometimes happens between two people. Things took a nasty turn, though, when one of the local hot shots leaned in and ran his hand up her leg without coming across with the necessary dough. Right away she acted offended, like where did he get the idea that she was that kind of girl, and she gave him a playful little slap.

"The guy immediately turned ugly and grabbed hold of her wrist like he was going to pull her down from the stage and do whatever the hell he wanted to do with her. So, because I've got this Sir Galahad streak in me, and since my first reaction to violence is violence, I stepped up behind the guy, wrapped my fingers around the back of his neck, and asked him politely if he had a problem with the young lady. He looked back at me with scared-rabbit eyes and assured me that he was just kidding, so I loosened my hold, nodded towards the door, and he very quickly scampered over to it and was gone without even a look back.

"That really impressed the GM execs. They respected me for being man enough to stick up for a woman, I guess, even though she was a stripper. The lady's chosen line of work didn't even enter into it for me, of course, but those guys weren't going to even get a clue to what that's all about at any time in their lives, know what I mean?"

"Yeah, I do," I said.

"The execs weren't the only ones who were impressed, though," he continued. "After I took care of the problem, the red-headed stripper got an eye-lock on me that wouldn't quit. She was breathing so hard they must have heard her at the top of the Ferris wheel. She was after my body big time, humping her hips to the music in my direction, darting her tongue in and out, licking her lips, that kind of thing. Needless to say, she had my complete attention.

"What could I do? There it was, staring me straight in the face. So I jumped up on the stage and picked her up by the waist and laid a smack-a-roo on her that she'd never forget. We kept right at it, too, just like we were alone somewhere. My hands crawling everywhere over her body, and she wasn't pulling away a bit, that's for sure. Of course, I'm a big ham, I love all the attention I can get, so I really got off on the crowd cheering me on. With all that encouragement, I wasn't about to limit my experience with the lady to semi-casual caresses.

"You've got to keep in mind that the female part of this act was naked at this point, except for her very feminine ruby-red slippers, and she was somewhat aggressively clawing at what she knew to be an especially sensitive part of my body. Let's just say that all systems were go, all the way. When she made a big show of jumping up and wrapping her legs around my waist, that was the limit for me. I could've consummated the relationship right there on stage, but somehow or other, I don't know, I ... wait, now, do you really want me to continue with this, or is it a bit too much?"

"Oh, I guess so, Jake, so what happened next?" I said in a nonchalant way, as if I really didn't care either way.

"Well," he laughed, "my date and I disappeared behind the curtain and did whatever for at least ten minutes. The guys out front were yelling so loud all through it that a couple of local cops who were assigned to the fair came into the tent to see what was the matter. When the cops yelled for us to come out from behind the curtain we did, of course, because I'm not a complete scofflaw, after all. I don't have to tell you what we did behind the curtain, do I, sir? You can imagine whatever you want to imagine, okay? You're pretty good at that anyway, right?"

"Yeah, Jake," I laughed, "okay, yeah. I'm pretty good at that."

"I'll just tell you that time with her behind the curtain was pretty close to being the most enjoyable ten minutes of my life, and we'll leave it at that." He went on, "There were times later on in life when I was in solitary confinement somewhere that I thought very fondly of that incident, I'll tell you. Anyway, after we were both completely satisfied, we walked out from behind the curtain hand-in-hand to center stage and did a series of courtly bows.

"Well, the proceedings made quite an impression on the GM execs in attendance, but the fallout from the little show the lady and I put on occurred rather soon thereafter, and it wasn't very positive. Evidently, when he got home to East Oshgosh one of the fucking pussies shared his account of the evenings activities with his loving wife, she repeated the details to the wife of one of the top executives of General Motors at a friggin' whist party or something, and ol' Jakie boy had his tenure with the company terminated. I guess the sales figures I generated got trumped by the exuberance of my extra-curricular activities. I was deemed to be bad for the company's image, and that was that.

"You know what, though? I didn't regret what I did one damn bit! That red-headed stripper was one helluva woman! Hell, I wouldn't trade that time behind the curtain with her for all the commission checks you could cram up the ass of that guy's mincy little wife in the course of a long, hot, summer afternoon in a pleasant suburb of Detroit!

"When you live life the way I do, you can't have any regrets. I don't get a fat retirement check from General Motors every month now, like I would have had I been better behaved, but I sure do have a lot of happy memories of those days, and that counts for something, right?"

"Yup," I said.

MIAMI BEACH

"After the General Motors fiasco, I was pretty much at a loss as to what I would do with the rest of my life. I was entirely aware that no one else on the face of the earth besides my mother gave a rat's ass what I did, and I knew she'd love and support me no matter what, so that gave me all the confidence I needed to accomplish whatever it might be that I set my mind to.

"We're talking early 1960s here. The whole country was churned up. Everything was being questioned. Drop out, turn on, all that horseshit. I wasn't about to

JAKE

Jake in Miami Beach with his red Triumph TR3

become a hippie, though, that's for damn sure, not after being a United States Army Airborne Para-trooper, and one hundred percent American all my

life. Hell, when I was six years old I wanted to donate my favorite toy truck to be melted down to a bullet to shoot up fucking Hitler's ass, oh, wait a minute, I already told you about that, right?"

"Yes, I think you did, Jake," I said.

"Anyway," he continued, "I was an American patriot right to the bone from the very beginning and that wasn't ever going to change. I sure as hell wasn't going to be marching in protest parades, and I also wasn't about to sign up to be a nine-to-fiver married to a wife who spent her afternoons in beauty parlors and her evenings watching television, expecting me to be on the couch next to her eating Freetos and clipping my toenails. The very thought of such a life gave me the heebie jeebies.

"Then out of nowhere, there it was. An absolutely beautiful deep red Triumph TR3 sports car that a buddy of mine sold to me for just about what I got in severance pay from General Motors. The first time I took it out for a spin I was in love, and I knew that it was my ticket to ride, ride, ride to wherever. And what better place for a wild and woolly young man on the loose to head to than Miami Beach, Florida? So there I go, whippin' down the East Coast towards all that sunshine and all those horny babes prancing around on the beach, just waiting for ol' Jakie boy to show up and they didn't even know it!

"As soon as I got to Miami, I got in touch with a paratrooper buddy by the name of Chris Kirkman, and he got me a job in a Miami Beach health club. That was big, very big. It was my first job in a health club and my introduction to a profession that would serve me well for the rest of my life. I've never done anything since in terms of gainful, serious employment but work in a health club, either as a trainer or manager. I've made a lot of money various other ways, you know what I mean, but I've never worked in any other field but health and fitness training since I got that first job in Miami Beach. Hey, what better way for someone to spend their time than working out and getting paid for it? Exercise is the natural way to stay high all the time and I've always been into it big time. And if there's anything I like better than feeling that natural high myself, it's turning someone else onto it, both men and women, old and young alike. Makes me feel like a friggin' evangelist or something.

"Here is the way, people! I've got the way! Let me take that body that the good Lord gave you and help you turn it into a source of everlasting joy!" he yelled, having a grand ol' time for himself, pumping his fists into the air and laughing his head off.

"The Miami Beach health club gig lasted for only about six months, actually," he said after a bit, "but it was very enjoyable and rewarding while it lasted. I got to work out and train others all day and had all the women I wanted at night. You have to keep in mind that it was 1961 and changes in society were taking place at a very rapid pace. All of a sudden what was forbidden before, wasn't now. I'll never forget those Miami Beach summer evenings, with the intoxicating aroma of tropical islands drifting across the water, and dozens of spoiled college girls from everywhere throwing off their tops and running along the warm sands with their long hair streaming behind them. Oh, liberation! Ain't it grand!

"Miami was great, but my paratrooper buddy Chris was always talking about going back to California, where the action really was, he said. More and better looking women than in Miami, of course, piles of money to be had, and the health club business was booming too. Hmmm ... after a while it all started to sound real good – hey, the whole country was California Dreamin' at the time anyway, that's definitely where it was happening – so we hopped into my Triumph one exceptionally sunny Miami afternoon, and started out on what would be my first trip across America, but not the last, by any means. Let me tell you about another ..."

"No, Jake," I said, "let's get you and your buddy out to California, if you don't mind."

"Right on!" he roared, thrusting his clenched fist up into the air.

*Hey, a guy's got to keep his car clean,
and it was too hot to wear a shirt!*

Jake, posing with his Triumph, fully loaded with all his and his friend Chris Kirkman's worldly possessions, moments before they headed out for California.

Chris Kirkman.

VOLUME ONE

THE BEAST FROM THE EAST

"So there I was in California, all alone, but not without direction. My ace in the hole in all this is that I had picked up the trade of fitness training in Miami, and California was just the place where it would prove to come in most handy. The health club business was booming, just like my friend Chris said it would be, and here was Mr. Jake on the scene, like icing on the cake. They welcomed me with open, well-developed arms, you might say.

"My big break came when I landed a gig at the Pasadena Vic Tanny Health Club, which at the time was the largest health club facility in the world. Vic had a number of health clubs all up and down the California coast at the time. He was very close friends with Jack LaLanne, and they were both absolute experts in the art of getting fit and staying that way. Jack and I saw eye-to-eye right from the beginning. He's been called 'The Godfather of Fitness' and the 'First Fitness Super-hero' and he deserves every bit of recognition he's ever gotten. Now here I am walking through the door, one muscular, crazy-eyed physical fitness guru, looking to get sweaty right along with the best of them. True believers spot one another right away and Vic hired me on the spot. He even re-did his brochures to announce my arrival on the scene. 'The Beast from The East' it said. I really liked that. I was very, very happy with the attention I was receiving. They had found the way to my heart.

"The greatest innovation Jack LaLanne brought to the health and fitness scene was providing females the opportunity to become physically fit right along with the men, and I was right with him on that one.

The world-famous physical fitness trainer Jack LaLanne in the early 1960s. Jack did a lot to help Jake convince Vic Tanny that weightlifting is as good for women as it is for men.

Unfortunately, Vic was still mired in the era when women lifting weights alongside men just didn't happen. Women were supposed to be purely ornamental, and any sign of muscular development on their bodies was a turn-off to all-American males. Vic was all for signing women up for memberships, of course, but he wanted their workouts to be restricted to roller machines and vibrator belts that would help them lose weight and tone up their bodies, not build muscle. He and I went round and round about his attitude in that regard, let me tell you, and he ended up almost firing me. What saved me was the fact that I was bringing in a record number of new members, both male and female. When Vic saw that women actually enjoyed lifting weights, and would pay to do so, he saw the light.

"Man, California was the place to be at the time! This was in the early sixties, before Hippies made their appearance, but there was already a definite buzz in the air, like something big was about to happen. Social customs were starting to change, big time. Long hair on men, women not shaving their legs and armpits, that sort of thing. Of course, I didn't go along with any of the anti-establishment stuff, I had been a U.S.Army paratrooper, don't forget, but there was an integrity about young people at the time that I respected, and I was enjoying the California scene very much."

"So, Jake, was this about the time you first met the Hell's Angels?" I asked him.

"No! And do not attempt to jump ahead of the story, sir!" he exploded. "I am leading us on a long and exciting journey that will get you where you want to go, have no doubt about that!"

Oddly enough, even though I wasn't, by any means, fully relaxed in Jake's presence at this point, I didn't get the fluttering in the stomach I might have earlier at such an outburst by him. I just calmly looked over at him and nodded my head, like I got the message, and asked him to continue as he wished.

"Vic was always trying to get me to open a location in any California city of my choosing," he continued, "and I was very tempted to take him up on it, because it meant I'd be making a lot more money and meeting even more interesting and attractive people, but, you know, I was getting lonesome for good ol' Maine. If you're not from Maine, you don't get it, I guess. Or maybe it's that I'm loyal to places in the same way I am to people, and I would have been lonesome for any place that was home, who knows? Anyway, after about two years, and without a lot of notice to anyone, I got into my 1950 faded green, four-door Plymouth sedan one fine California morning and headed out across the country, back home to Maine."

"That was in November of 1961, when I was twenty-three years old. And just to satisfy your need to know, my friend, I will tell you that I returned to California a few years later and became a member of the Hell's Angels Motorcycle Club at that time, but we have a ways to go yet before we get there, okay?"

"Yeah, okay, thank you," I said.

DEATH VALLEY

"The trip across America back to Maine went pretty much without incident, except for my almost freezing to death in Death Valley, that is. The incident is very pertinent to my relationship with my guardian angel and with the Hell's Angels Motorcycle Club, therefore I shall relate it to you in some detail.

"I am very big on America, as I have mentioned to you now and then, and I have always had the desire to visit as many national landmarks as possible, so it occurred to me to take a slight detour to Death Valley on the way home. It was scorching hot when I arrived, and after driving a while with the sun streaming through the windshield into my eyes, I decided to pull over into a rest area to get some sleep in the back seat. Curling up in the back seat felt good, and I fell right off to sleep, but when I woke up a few hours later in the wee hours of the morning I was so cold I couldn't move. My whole body felt pleasantly numb and I just wanted to go fall back into a long, restful sleep. Ah, now I know how the place got its name, I remember thinking. I later learned that people don't normally wake up when they're freezing to death in their sleep, they just kind of float peacefully off into eternity. That's why they say freezing to death is the best way to go. Something woke me up and kept me awake, though, and I knew without a doubt that it was my guardian angel. I had felt her warm and gentle presence at other times of crisis in my life, so it was a very familiar feeling to me.

"As I lay there, half trying to fully wake up, I became conscious of a battle going on for my soul. My guardian angel was gently tugging at me, urging me to sit up, but there were entities I knew to be angels from the dark side hovering over me and murmuring that I should give in to my desire to go into a deep and peaceful sleep. The angels from the dark side said they knew from the time I stabbed that guy, then jumped up onto that rock on the beach and yelled 'I am the Angel from Hell!' that I was one of them and now it was time for me to come home with them. They led me through the major events of my life up to that point, praising me for all the wonderful things I had accomplished. They showed me the happy faces of people I had helped throughout my life. They assured me that those who I loved and who meant the most to me – my mother and the close friends I had made – wouldn't need my help anymore because of all the wonderful things I had done for them in the past. It would please them all very much if I took a long and peaceful rest, they told me. It was my destiny from birth to rule in Hell, they said, and they assured me that I would have a high standing among them, and the only thing I had to do was let go of this life to be happy with them for eternity.

"I was drawn first to one side, then to the other. It was the very battle that had been raging inside me all of my life. Somehow or other, though, through it all, I knew the final decision to choose between remaining in this life, or stepping over into the dark side, would be mine, that I was free to choose either way.

"My great love for this life won out! I'd always lived my life with great passion, and I'd loved every minute of it! The good times and the bad! So, yes! I chose life! I even friggin' yelled it out! 'I choose life! I choose life!' I screamed, but man did I have to fight to stay alive! I kept trying to move parts of my body, first my fingers, then my hands and wrists, then when I tried to lift my knee and it moved I yelled 'I choose life!' again. That's wehn the angels from hell fluttered away and I felt only the warm presence of my guardian angel.

"It was still very cold in the car, of course, and I sat there for at least an hour, forcing myself to stretch, even though it was painful as hell. It was one of the hardest physical ordeals I've ever gone through in my life, and all I was trying to do was sit up in the back seat of a car! Every moment of this life counts for a great deal, my friend, and we have to always remember to be grateful for it!"

"Yep," I said.

"I'll never forget the sight of that gigantic Death Valley blazing sun appearing over the horizon as I sat there in that back seat feeling the warmth come over me and getting my energy back. I became overwhelmed at how incredibly and absolutely wonderful this life is! I felt a glow around me that I feel right now when I think of sitting there in the back seat of my Plymouth that morning! Man, was I happy to be alive! And I still am! You'd better believe it!

"How ironic! I pushed those angels from the dark side away that night in Death Valley, even though I had declared myself to be one of them at a very young age. Keep in mind also, sir, that the time hadn't come yet when I would realize my destiny by becoming a member of the Hell's Angels Motorcycle Club. I hadn't even heard of them at the time! We are on a long strange journey, my friend!"

We're on a long strange journey. Those very words were graffitied in big letters on the masonry at the top of a building in downtown Portland for years. No one ever bothered to remove them, for some reason. I asked Jake if he was the one who graffitied it up there and he was absolutely flabbergasted that I would accuse him of such an outrageous act.

"You talking about *me* doing something like that?!" he yelled, laughing his head off.

Okay, so I had my answer.

FIVE

Jake and I were getting along very well by this time, and I was becoming more and more relaxed in his presence. So much so that I started to get a little lax in arriving at his apartment on time for our interviews. You know, a half-hour or so late, fairly regularly. It wasn't a big deal to me, and I didn't think it was for him, but I found out differently when I arrived about a half-hour late this time.

"What the fuck?!" he roared. "What the hell is wrong with you?! You're late every damn time! Are you trying to friggin' disrespect me?! How about if I pick you up and throw you out the fucking window?!"

He was serious. Oh, maybe not about throwing me out the window, I guess, but he damn well got the message across that he was more than a little annoyed with me.

"Okay, Jake, I get the point," I said. "I'll be on time from now on."

I couldn't quite believe it, but I wasn't scared. A little concerned, maybe, but not scared. When we first met, just being in his presence had given me the jitters, now he was screaming in my face and I was calm on the inside. Exactly why, I didn't know, but that's the way it was.

He calmed down to a low growl after a bit, and I even spotted a quick smile. He had detected the change in me and was pleased to see it.

"So, buddy boy," he said, laughing now, "what is on our agenda today?"

"Okay, Jake! Let's get to it!" I commanded him, chuckling along with him at my newfound way of being. "That Death Valley thing you told me last time about the battle for your soul between the forces of good and evil and how your guardian angels led you to the light was quite a tale," I said. "It must have made a big difference in the way you looked at life from then on, right?"

After smirking a bit, he started speaking very slowly and precisely, trying to be patient with me: "Naw, it didn't change me all that much, I just got a little more so, know what I mean? My first and only priority has always been to try to live each moment to the fullest and the experience in Death Valley reinforced that big time. Face every circumstance head on, be who you are, own up to it all, go for the gusto every time, and you'll have one helluva ride. You know what I mean?"

I nodded over to him, like sure I do, that's the way I live too, sort of.

"After my soul wrenching experience in Death Valley," he said sarcastically, looking over me and grinning, "I set out upon a contemplative journey across America and ended up spending some time at a Trappist Monastery somewhere in... Nooo! Just kidding!" he laughed. The odd part is that I was believing every word of it.

"The truth is that I did kind of get stalled here and there on the way home, but the diversions I ran into were more of a carnal nature, if you get my drift. I was the new guy in town wherever I happened to stop, twenty-three years old, standin' tall an' lookin' good, with a good supply of spending money in my jeans and driving a snappy vehicle, so there you go. Let's just say that a lot of very interesting ladies along the way gave me plenty of good reason to want to remain in their presence, but I had a hunger to get back to Maine, and that was it.

"Oh," he said, "okay, maybe I'll tell you about a little

afternoon delight I experienced in a small town out-side of Toledo, I, ah ..."

"No, Jake," I said, interrupting him, "let's get you back to Portland. I can imagine what I want to about what took place on the particular afternoon, know what I mean?"

"Oh yeah, I forget how good you are at that kind of thing!" he roared, cracking me up.

"Let's just get you back to Maine!" I yelled, after I stopped laughing.

Jake bought this 1940 Ford two-door sedan in 1961 for $75 when he got back to Portland from California. He says he made some body and mechanical changes that transformed it into a very cool hot rod. The 1950 Cadillac engine he installed helped out a lot in drag races.

VOLUME ONE

THE PORTLAND HEALTH STUDIO
AND FIGURE SALON

"I got back to good ol' Portland in the fall of 1961," he resumed, "and I was very happy to be home! No matter where I've been around the country, or what I was involved in, I always knew that I'd return to Portland someday. Although I was brought up in an affluent neighborhood across the bay in South Portland, by the time I was in my early teens I had developed a fascination for the streets of Portland and headed across the bridge every chance I got. As soon as I made contact with some inner-city neighborhood kids across the bridge, that was the world I was interested in belonging to. Where that came from in me exactly, I don't know, but there it is. So now, there I was, back in Portland. The Miami Beach party boy and California dreamin' health and fitness guru was back in town!

"Yeah, I was all set to go alright, but I knew I needed to make a living one way or another. As I have told you, I knew when I began training people in Miami Beach that I would work in the field of health and physical fitness for the rest of my life so, after having done just that in California, my intention was to apply for a job at a Portland health club. I discovered that there wasn't even a health club in Portland at the time, though, so I very reluctantly applied for a position at the YMCA. They were blown away by my resumé, and I was very close to being hired as a trainer in their fitness program, but I really didn't want to go that route. The YMCA fitness program wasn't quite my speed, as you can imagine.

"Then, out of nowhere, I heard about two guys from Boston who owned a couple of health clubs down there and were looking to open one up in Portland. I scouted them out real quick and they were delighted to make my acquaintance and enter into a mutually satisfactory business arrangement. They had struck gold when they met me, and they knew it. Not only was I a local boy with a fantastic physique and oddly entertaining ways, I also had an impressive resumé as a health and fitness trainer, with a signed glowing recommendation by Vic Tanny, who at the time was the biggest star in America's exploding health and fitness industry. Those guys couldn't believe their good fortune when I walked through the door!

"Tra-la-la, ladies and gentlemen," Jake announced with a grand sweep of his arm, "let me introduce you to The Portland Health Studio and Figure Salon, located right in the middle of town, the first health club, not only in Portland, but in the entire state of Maine! And the wildest and most exciting part is that Portland Health and Fitness Salon is managed by Portland's returned prodigal son, good ol' Jonathan 'Jake' Sawyer!"

"Just by coincidence, the location we decided on for the health club was on Center Street, on the second and third floors up over the original DiMillo's Restaurant, and right across the street from Sawyer-Barker, the clothing manufacturing company I've told you about that my family had owned for a number of generations. I had a lot of good memories of working at Sawyer-Barker as a teenager, and when the employees found out that I was managing a health club right across the street they were all excited about coming over to visit me. We had some great ol' times reminiscing about my shady past – which was only about five years previous! Imagine how the legends have grown in the sixty years since then!

"Anyway, The Portland Health Studio and Figure Salon was a huge success right from the very beginning. We made fitness fashionable in Portland. All of a sudden it was okay for businesspeople to be seen carrying a gym bag. Weightlifting wasn't just for assorted lunkheads and self-obsessed body builders anymore.

"A very important part of the scene I'm describing to you is that we made it acceptable for women to lift weights. You, of course, recall what I told you about the innovations Jack LaLanne and Vic Tanny and I had made in that regard when I worked for Vic in California. Well, the attitude concerning women lifting weights was even more antagonistic in Maine than it was in California, as you might imagine would have been the case. I blew a hole right through that nonsense right away, though. I made the public aware that working out is good for *every* body, and that we welcomed women and treated them with proper respect. The ladies also knew that I was ready and able to deal with the 'starers.' It was natural and quite expected that males would glance now and then, but the women we wanted as members weren't interested in becoming objects of interest, and I always enjoyed taking googly-eyed male offenders by the ear and leading them over to and out the door.

"I also stressed the need for all the members to follow an overall fitness plan including, of course, paying proper attention to their dietary intake, and that's where ol' Jakie boy's personally developed 'California Hi-Protein' health drink came in. It contained generous proportions of powdered eggs and milk, plus beet sugar, and a secret ingredient that I refused to

JAKE

Jake's good friend and training instructor, Fran, poses with the ever-popular vibrator belt machines, at the Portland Health Club and Figure Salon in 1962. Jake says he spray-painted the machines a bright, shiny gold to add some California sunshine to the place.

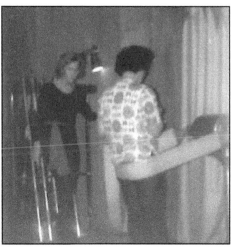

A female client using a vibrator belt, under Fran's strict supervision. What more could a lady ask for?

divulge, even to my closest friends and associates.

Suffice it to say that my miracle elixir contained all of the amino acids necessary for the body to assimilate the powerful proteins contained in the mixture, and that those who made 'California Hi-Protein' part of a well-balanced diet experienced optimal health and happiness. Those who needed to lose weight did, and those who wanted to add weight did that as well, and it was mostly due to my secret ingredient.

"Let me tell you a story that will make clear to you exactly what the secret ingredient to my super-drink was ..."

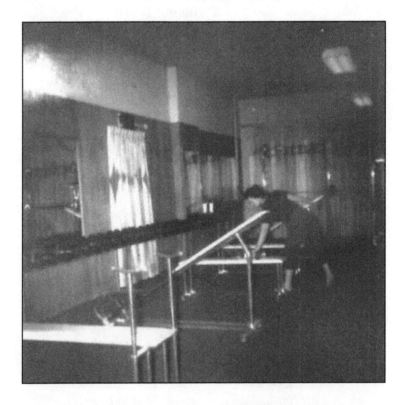

The Portland Health Club and Figure Salon featured wall-to-wall red carpeting, like Jake had seen in the Vic Tanny clubs in California.

JAKE

"Okay, Jake," I said, "just this once, but then, after that, let's get back to The Portland Health and Fitness Salon, okay?"

"Yes, sir," he said, snapping me a smart military salute.

"Some years after I managed the Portland Health and Fitness Salon and developed my California Hi-Protein drink," he began, "when I found myself incarcerated at San Quentin prison, I was able to acquire the necessary ingredients for my special elixir through the underground prison system, and I ran a very brisk business selling my miracle elixir to the members of the weightlifting club I started in the prison. Somehow or other, maybe it was something I said, I can't really recall exactly, the guys came to believe that if they wanted to put on a serious amount of new muscle, they weren't going to do so with the meager amount of protein we were given in our prison meals. It was very important for us to be big and strong, after all, because we were members of a group I founded named 'The Regulators' for the purpose of settling whatever disputes and disagreements might arise among the San Quentin prison population that wanted to kill us. We expected to be generously compensated for our negotiating services, of course, by any and all involved on either side of the issue. As you can imagine, The Regulators had to be in the best of shape for all of this peace keeping, and California Hi-Protein became an essential part of our health and fitness program.

"I refused, of course, like I had when I managed the Portland Health and Fitness Studio, to divulge the secret ingredient in California Hi-Protein to anyone at San Quentin. There was this one guy, though, who wanted very badly to take over my extremely profitable business after I got paroled, and he kept at me about it so much that I promised him I'd tell him the secret ingredient on the day I walked out the door of the prison. He could hardly wait, so that made two of us. Then, when the big day came, he came up to me all excited with a pen and a little notebook ready to take down the name of the secret ingredient.

"'Okay, Jake, you said you were going to tell me the secret ingredient of California Hi-Protein today!' he said.

"I was in a really good mood that day, as you might imagine, so I was as kind and generous to him as I could be. I gave him a big, happy smile and a pat on the back and said: 'The secret ingredient of California Hi-Protein is to have faith in your product! Believe in it yourself, that will make other people believe in it, and miracles will happen! They will gain weight! They will lose weight! Whatever they believe will happen, will happen!'

"The guy's face dropped like he didn't know what the hell I was getting at, and he walked away hanging his head. I heard somewhere later that the venture bottomed out for him before long, but that someone else with a more positive attitude who had more of an understanding of what salesmanship is all about had started selling California Hi-Protein again, and they did really well at it. To tell you the truth, I wouldn't be surprised to find out that California Hi-Protein is still being made and sold at San Quentin today by some enterprising individual. That's quite a legacy, huh?"

"Yea, sure Jake," I said, "but let's get back to what went on in Portland with you after you got back from the West Coast."

"You've got it!" he said, obviously pleased with my new, assertive attitude.

JAKE

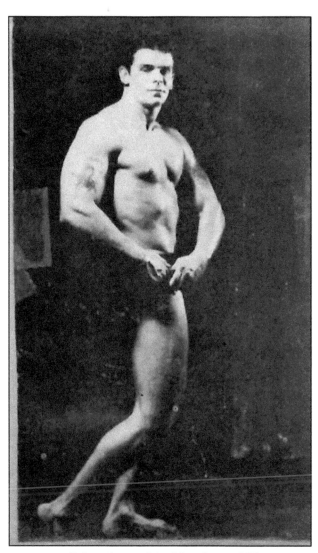

Jake pictured in Muscle and Fitness
Magazine, October, 1962

*Jake in his doctor's smock, upstairs over Portland's
first health club, creating California High Protein.*

*Grand Opening day at the
Lewiston Health and Fitness Salon.*

JAKE

THE LEWISTON HEALTH STUDIO
AND FIGURE SALON

"The Portland Health and Fitness Salon was going so well in Portland that we decided to open another salon in Lewiston," Jake continued. "I found us a location in the middle of the downtown, at 1119 Lisbon Street, and right away we were the biggest news in town. To begin with, one of the owners had a brand new Jaguar XKE that he gave me liberal use of, and when I parked that beauty out in front of the salon our image was made. A car like that was big stuff in Lewiston, Maine. Memberships rolled in and, with the orders I was getting from both clubs, I had all I could do to keep up with the production of California Hi-Protein."

At this point Jake pulled a photo album down from a shelf and showed me a copy of the newspaper ad he ran in the local papers for the two health clubs. There he was, back in 1962, twenty-four years old, handsome as hell, in the classic strongman pose, wearing the smile of a contented man who's got it made in every way, and is entirely aware of it.

We were nearing the end of our allotted time together and, given the way that things had started out that day, I wanted to be sure we ended the session on an agreeable note, so I said: "Jake, how about telling me the funniest story you can remember from around that time?"

He sat there for a moment with his chin in his hand, musing to himself, and I could see that he was sifting through a number of different stories he might tell me. He'd periodically chuckle and shake his head no, but then he brightened up like he'd found a good one for sure.

Jake with the 1961 Jaguar one of the Boston owners of the Portland and Lewiston Health and Fitness Salons let him use to travel between the two cities. Jake says he hit 130 mph quite regularly cruising down the Maine Turnpike.

The man, Lewiston, 1963

Jake says it sook some strategic photo cropping to achieve the narrow waist pictured here. He also says he never even entered the Mr. California competition, much less won it – but that the ad was very effective!

Jake posing for a magazine photo at the Lewiston Health Club and Figure Salon in 1963. He says he posed so that his back would be reflected in the mirror behind him.

The staff of the Lewiston Health and Fitness Salon.

Instructors Fran and Donna pose in front of the sign Jake designed. Jake was proud of the sign, he says, because it brought in a lot of new clients and cost him next to nothing to erect, inasmuch as he paid the sign company off with three club memberships and two late-model Cadillacs, which he says he acquired through the "100% Discount, no money put down by me" system he had developed years before.

JAKE

DRINKING COW'S BLOOD

"Okay, here ya go," he said. "I laugh every time I think of this one myself, so maybe you'll appreciate it. It's about the time my ol' weight-lifting buddy Bruce Chambers and I drank cow's blood because we had it on good authority that it would make us stronger.

"The story starts back when I was managing the Vic Tanny Health Club in Pasadena. There were a lot of celebrities who came through the door of the club, but the one I remember best is Archie Moore, the great middleweight boxing champion. He liked working out with us because I kept him laughing. When he went to other places, the trainers were so thrilled to have him in their place they were uptight around him. *Mr. Moore* this, *Mr. Moore*, that. Hell, I called him Archie right from the beginning and offered to set him up with a nice little white college girl if he wanted, or even with a tight-assed frat boy from U.C.L.A., if that was his preference. That really broke him up.

"Anyway, Archie really got a kick out of me. He was amused by the way I was always looking for ways to get stronger, and he had all kinds of suggestions for me. One day he took me aside and put his hand on my arm and whispered that he'd tell me something if I promised to keep it to myself. I agreed, of course.

"He told me that the secret to his success is that he drinks cow's blood. The fresher the better. No boiling it before drinking it, or anything like that. He said he learned about drinking cow's blood from an African tribal chieftain years ago on a trip to the land of his ancestors, and that it's what made him a champion. Before he started drinking cow's blood his boxing career was kind of stalling, he said, but drinking cow's blood kicked it into high gear.

"Okay now, one of my all-time most favorite weight-lifting buddies in Portland while I was managing the club there was a guy named Bruce Chambers. He was a friggin' animal. Weighed over three-hundred pounds and was all muscle. He had a warm heart, despite his menacing appearance, but like me, he loved to fight and would do anything to get stronger so he could fight better.

"One of the things you find out when you lift weights is that at some point you seem to hit a brick wall. At first you grow and grow, but after a while you don't see any change no matter how hard you work out. It can become frustrating as hell and you'll do anything to experience the kind of growth you had in the beginning.

Bruce Chambers

JAKE

"I owe all I have to weight training," says big Jake Sawyer, who operates the Lewiston Health Studio in Lewiston, Maine. Seven years ago spinal surgery left him weighing 144 at 6'2". Weights built him up, allowed him to play college football. He weighs 218 pounds in this photo, with 18½" biceps and 48½" chest.

Strength and Health Magazine, December 1963.

"A lot of the guys were getting into steroids, and that kind of shit, but I've always kept it honest, mostly. It's me and the weights. No intermediary bullshit. Drugs are for slugs, I've always said. When Bruce started fretting about not getting bigger and stronger no matter what he did, though, I remembered what Archie told me about drinking cow's blood, and when I told Bruce about what Archie told me, he was into it all the way. He felt great mentally and physically, and was beginning to get somewhere in weightlifting competition, but no matter how hard he worked his body wouldn't grow any more. Bring on the cow's blood! So I looked in the phone book and found out that there was a slaughter house out on Presumpscot Street, not too far from downtown Portland, and Bruce and I couldn't wait to go out there.

"When the supervisor of the place saw two humongous weightlifters walking through the door and I told him what we were after he about fell on the floor laughing his ass off. He kept asking me over and over if I was serious, so finally I told him what Archie Moore had told me. That got him laughing like a bastard again, but after he got himself together a little he said for us to follow him into the next room where his crew was on break. He had me repeat to the crew why Bruce and I were there, and when I did they acted like this was the greatest entertainment they'd had standing up in a long, long time. I guess not that much happens in a slaughterhouse on a day-to day basis, after all.

"One of the guys gave Bruce a bucket and told us to follow him, so we did, with the rest of the crew following right behind us, having a great time poking each other in the ribs and giggling like little girls, like they just couldn't wait for the action to get underway.

"When we got to where the room where cow's that were on death row were kept, the guys who gave Bruce the bucket made a big show of letting us choose the cow we wanted slaughtered, and they told us all about the spirit and personality of this and that cow because we told them that Archie said that cow's blood had a big effect on you psychologically, made you more aggressive and manly, according to the personality of the cow, so obviously you wanted to choose the most spirited one of the bunch.

"So we took our time deciding, with the crew acting just as serious about it as we were, and after we had finally made our choice, one of the guys threw a rope around the poor thing's neck and led it over to the other side of the room, where the slaughtering area was.

"What a brutal fucking operation! Bruce and I thought of ourselves as being real tough guys who could take anything, but we weren't quite ready for this. Right away the guy wraps a long chain around the cow's back legs, hits a switch, and the cow gets yanked up by the ass-end and hangs there upside down, mooing its fucking heart out.

"Stand over here with the bucket!" the guy yells at Bruce, then he picks up a meat cleaver, and after making a big show of running his thumb along the cutting edge to test it for sharpness, he takes a helluva whack at the cow's throat.

"Blood gushes out like a friggin' dam had burst, and Bruce jumps back, horrified as hell, but the guy motions for him to step up and hold the bucket under the cow's throat to catch the blood. So Bruce kind of stumbles forward and holds the bucket at arm's length under the fucking flowing blood, looking over at me like he's thinking maybe we should get the hell out of there and call the whole thing a draw.

"He stuck with it though, and after the bucket got filled up the whole crew started cheering like ol' Bruce had just scored a touchdown in the big game or something. Bruce stands there holding the bucket full of blood smiling broadly, of course, because he likes any kind of recognition.

"So then we all trooped back into the other room and the crew gathered around us waiting for us to take a drink of the blood. We had made the mistake of telling them that Archie said it had to be fresh cow's blood to have the desired effect, so we had to drink some of it right then.

"I had my doubts about whether I could pull that off, I really did, after the brutality of the slaughter and everything, the romance was wearing off. Added to everything else is that fresh blood from any frigging mammal has an odor that is very unpleasant. The crew was used to it, of course, but I was starting to feel a little queasy and my mind was working overtime trying to figure a way out of this.

"Bruce wasn't into it all that much either, you could tell by the way he kept glancing at the door and then looking over to me with his brow all wrinkled up. But when one of the crew suggested that Bruce might be chicken to drink some of the cow's blood, that was it. Bruce wasn't about to be called chicken any time about anything. So up went the bucket to his mouth and he took a helluva long drink.

"When he lowered the bucket, his face was all white and he just kept staring straight ahead all beady eyed, like something was going on in his stomach that was confusing the hell out of him.

"*Aw shit*, I said to myself, *my turn.*

"There was just no getting out of it, so I grabbed the bucket from Bruce and held it up to my mouth. I didn't take a drink, I just couldn't bring myself to do it, but when one of the guys yelled that he wasn't seeing my Adams apple move up and down like I was drinking, I knew I had to suck it up and take a drink.

"That stuff tasted so fucking bad I can still taste it today. I thought at the time that it was going to destroy my appetite for eating or drinking anything ever again for the rest of my life.

"Bruce wasn't saying or doing a damn thing. He was just standing there, looking straight ahead with a blank look on his face. He drank a lot more than I did, so I can imagine what he felt like.

"The guys were laughing so hard they were falling over each other and leaning up against the walls for support.

"'How'd you like it? How'd you like it?' they kept asking us.

"'Great! Great!' we said.

"'Hey, do you have a jar we can put some of this in so we can have more later?' I asked.

"'Sure!' one of them yelled, then scurried to another room and came back with a big jar and filled it up with blood from the bucket.

"'A little something for the road!' he said as he handed me the jar.

"I took the jar and we said our goodbyes, then I threw the fucking thing away as soon as we were out the door. I knew for sure the crew was watching through the window, but by that time I didn't give a shit either way.

"I have to say that neither one of us felt any stronger after drinking cow's blood. In fact, we felt weak as kittens for quite a while. That stuff raises hell with your digestive system. And it's not like they make a special medicine to treat people who make the mistake of drinking fresh cow's blood. You just kind of have to wait until the effects wear off by themselves.

"Archie Moore is gone now, but I just know he's up there in the big ring in the sky somewhere, leaning back against the ropes laughing himself silly, thinking about those two dumb-ass white boys down there drinking fresh cow's blood, because he told them it would make them bigger and stronger.

"Hey, I've been called a genius," Jake said, "but no one ever said I had any sense!"

Archie Moore (Public Domain photo)

JAKE

Jake astride his first motorcycle, a 1952 Harley-Davidson, which he bought for $350 cash at a used car lot up in Naples, Maine, a small town about 35 miles west of Portland. He says he had never ridden a motorcycle before, but when he saw that Harley it was love at first sight. When I asked him how he got it home, Jake laughed like hell and gave me my answer: "I rode it home! What the hell do you think I was going to do, walk beside it and wheel it? Learning to ride that Harley on my trip home from Naples was an experience that will live with me for the rest of my life! None of the wild-assed, death-defying things I've done on a motorcycle since have even come close to being as fucking insane and thrilling to the core of my being as that trip home that day! When I finally figured out how to control that baby, I felt like I was master of the planet! I had united with a force I hadn't even known existed and was off and running to a lifetime of being totally in love with motorcycles!"

SIX

I could see that Jake was pleased when I showed up at his apartment about ten minutes early for this session. After the fireworks last time about my habitual tardiness, I was damn sure going to be on time from now on. He had interpreted my lateness as disrespect for him, and I wasn't about to fall back into my dangerous habits. This time I got to his building a half-hour early and sat in the lobby for fifteen minutes before I went up on the elevator. Arriving too early would have amounted to ass-kissing, and he wouldn't have liked that, while showing up even a little late would have been too damn late for my own good.

"So everything was peachy for you upon your return home in the early 60s, Jake," I said, getting right to it after we got settled in our chairs across from one another. "Business was booming at the health clubs in Portland and Lewiston, California Hi-Protein was selling like mad, and I'm sure you had a very active sex life, being in the primo physical condition you were, and with all those lovely Portland ladies to choose from. Then there were the high ol' times you were having with all the buddies you had in low places all around town, getting into all kinds of mischief. Things were hummin' along pretty well all-around, huh?"

BOOM! FATE INTERVENES!

"Yeah, everything was going just great at that time," he answered, "my life was buzzing along so nicely that the thought of leaving Maine again never even oc-curred to me. I had been around the country a good deal and had had a bang-up ol' time wherever I went, but now I was home where I belonged and lovin' every minute of it. I was happier and more content than I had ever been in my life, to tell you the truth, but out of nowhere, I went from on top of the world to deep down in a black hole looking up, desperately hoping to see just a glimmer of light up there.

"All this grief had to do with a near-fatal motorcycle accident I had in the fall of 1963, when I was twenty-five years old. It happened up in Lewiston as I was getting on the turnpike to go down to Portland. I was in my glory going back and forth between the health clubs on the turnpike on my Harley, with that king of the road attitude you know, passing everything in sight, getting from one place to the other in record time which, of course, meant that each time I was trying to break my own speed record. The State Police would see me whiz by, or think they did, but I swear I never got pulled over in all that time. Pure luck, I guess. Ironically, though, the cause of the accident was not excessive speed.

"I was on an access road to the turnpike, stopped at a light in the left lane of traffic, about three car lengths to the rear of a car sitting in the right lane up at the light. Experienced motorcyclists like myself like to have that space between them and the light so that they can start their forward motion before the light changes and be up to it at a good rate of speed just as it turns green, thereby positioning themselves to be out ahead of the line of traffic. The dangerous part of that practice, though, is that automobile drivers often neglect to look back through their side view mirror for approaching motorcycles before they turn left. It's actually the most common cause of automobile-motorcycle accidents, and the most preventable, if only motorists would get a life and look through their side view mirror before they make a sharp left turn! Anyway, I was up to almost full throttle when I got up to the light and this asshole turned left directly in front of me! Boom!

"I swerved to the left, thereby avoiding full frontal impact with the car, which undoubtedly saved my life, but because I had to stand up to avoid my whole body being slammed into the side of the car, I was thrown off the bike upon impact and was shot like a cannon ball across the hood. I flew for fifteen or twenty yards through the air before I crash landed on the road, then rolled over and over for about that same distance before ending up in a ditch, wondering what the fuck had just happened.

"I was in a world of hurt. I had so many life-threatening injuries and had lost so much blood that the doctors said that I probably wouldn't have made it if I wasn't in such great physical shape. I suffered a serious concussion, a broken right arm, and two fractured ribs on my right side. But the worst damage was to my right leg, I had shattered my right femur so severely that the doctors said it would definitely have to be taken off. What made things even worse, the doctors told me, was that my right femur bone was splintered and crushed so badly that there wasn't enough stump left to attach an artificial leg to. So what that meant was that I was going to have a very short stump where my right leg had been, and for the rest of my life I would either be in a wheelchair or walking on crutches.

"Man, all that bad news hit me very hard! I was twenty-five years old and active as hell, man! I was bursting with life and striding good ol' Mother Earth like a friggin' giant on steroids! And now this!

"Let's come up with something here, men!" I screamed at the doctors, which caused them to go into a big huddle to discuss the situation. When they broke up the lead surgeon pulled up a chair and sat next to the bed and asked me very seriously if I was willing to undergo a long-shot experimental procedure that would entail a painful operation, which would be followed by a long recovery period filled with great pain and discomfort, with not a lot of hope that the procedure would be at all successful.

"'Hell yes!' I yelled, 'let's get on with it! Sounds great to me!'"

MAKING MEDICAL HISTORY

"The procedure entailed inserting a one-foot-long, one-half-inch in diameter, stainless steel metal rod into the center of my femur bone, with the hope that cartilage would form around it, at which point the rod would be removed and, hopefully, cartilage would continue to form and eventually fill in the space where the rod had been. Essentially, they were betting on the bone's ability to rebuild itself.

"Keep in mind here, my friend, that we're talking 1963. The procedure was like science fiction then. The doctors told me that what they proposed to do had never been attempted before, and they were very careful to warn me against harboring false hope.

"'False hope?!' I roared at them, 'False hope seems to be the only hope I've got! So get your jackknives out and let's get at it!'

"They put me out for the operation, of course, but

when I woke up I was in more pain than I ever knew existed.

The recovery period was every bit as painful as they said it would be, especially the first couple of months, when my femur bone and leg muscles were making friends with the steel rod. Keep in mind that I was also dealing with the remnants of a pretty severe concussion at the time, as well as a broken right arm and two fractured ribs, so I'd had better times in my life. It wasn't fun, I'll tell you that, but at least I was alive.

"I went through some heavy shit, man. Mental as well as physical. All through it I knew that there was a fairly good chance that my body would reject the steel rod and all the pain and anguish I'd gone through wouldn't count for a damn thing.

"There was a delicate balance that had to be arrived at, whereby I had to be gentle with my body and allow it to heal, while at the same time moving and exercising my muscles so that they would grow and become strong again. My natural impulse, of course, is to go right for it, dig in and throw everything I've got into achieving my goal, but this time I had to arrive at a happy balance. The ying and the yang, you know, that kind of thing. Yeah, right, like that's going to happen with me. The truth is, I said the hell with the ying and the yang stuff and went right the fuck for it, like I've always done. 'Pain means healing, pain means healing,' I'd say over and over to myself, so bring it on!

"Let me interject here, sir, that one very positive development at that particular time was my meeting an absolutely beautiful blonde RN at the hospital named Barbara, who became the love of my life. She was not only a highly trained nurse who provided me with the best of medical care, she also provided me with an abundance of love and affection throughout the two-year recovery period. You know what having a good woman in your corner means, right?"

"Yeah, I do," I said, "I sure do."

"For the first few weeks after the operation, sharp pain shot through my entire body whenever I tried to move my right leg even slightly," Jake continued, "but I kept at it, and after a while the pain was only on the right side, then only in the right hip and leg. As time went on, I could actually take a short walk with not a lot of pain, and after about a year I could swing my right leg up onto my Harley without experiencing excruciating pain. The pain was still there, no question, but I had made friends with it, sort of. We had come to this gentleman's agreement that it would go away altogether if I just went about my business like I'd always done. Pain is inevitable, suffering is optional, so let's get on with the show!

"Needless to say, I was completely gratified when the steel rod was removed, which was two years from the time it was inserted. It was determined that the technique had been a great success. The initial operation and the two-year healing period, with all the pain and discomfort I went through, had been damn well worth it. Since that time, I've had to wear the orthopedic shoe you see right here," he said, slapping the side of his right shoe, "and, of course, I'd acquired the trademark lurch that strikes fear into the hearts of bad guys everywhere, but other than that I was the same ol' Jakie boy, up an' at 'em once again!

"It might interest you to know that I taped the steel rod that was in my femur bone for those two years onto the right fork of my Harley, as you can see illustrated in that picture taken at the time," he said, grinning broadly and pointing to a picture of himself straddling his Harley more than fifty years ago. Sure

Jake on his Harley. The six-inch long steel rod that was used to fuse the bones of his right leg to his femur bone, and was in his body for a year and a half, is mounted at the top of the right fork of the bike.

enough, when I studied the picture, there it was, the steel rod that had been in his leg for two years, strapped at the top of the fork of his Harley.

I looked over at his right foot and shook my head in disbelief. In all this time, I hadn't noticed that he wears an orthopedic shoe! His right shoe has a very high built-up sole, which he says is due to the fact that his right leg is almost two-inches shorter than his left leg, and I had made the same false assumption that everyone else has been making over the years. Turns out that his lurching gate is largely due to his physical condition, not to any intention on his part to intimidate one and all.

"Jake," I said, looking over at him very seriously. "You're telling me that you've worn that orthopedic shoe since you had that steel rod removed, more than fifty years ago? All the wild and crazy things you've done since that time, all the fights, becoming a Hell's Angel, riding your motorcycle back and forth across the country a few times, going to various jails and prisons, all the things you did to get there, and all the other insane, wild-ass stuff you've done over the past fifty or so years, that all took place *after* you had your right leg almost completely torn off at the hip and the doctors said you'd never walk on two legs ever again in your life?"

Jake, still on crutches, astride the Harley he was in the accident with. The front-end of the bike was torn, he says, so he had some repairing to do.

"You're getting the picture, my man," he said, chuckling. "I told you at the very beginning of this little project we're involved in here that I had made a decision at a very early age to go right straight for the gusto under any and all circumstances, throughout my entire life, did I not? Did I say anything about exceptions having to do with major injuries or anything of that nature?"

"No," I said, "but I ..."

"Contained in the medical archives of Maine Medical Center is a ground-breaking case history with my name on it, sir. They told me that my case was unique in the annals of orthopedic surgery, and I have always been very pleased to know that I've done my part to enhance the quality and effectiveness of the treatment a person receives today when they've had an accident similar to the one I had.

"It's not what happens to us that matters, my friend," he continued, "things will always happen to us, for good or for bad, it's our reaction to what happens that matters. It's what we do with what happens to us that determines our fate. I didn't enjoy what happened to me one bit, believe me. I was in friggin' pain for so long sometimes I thought I was either going to jump off the highest bridge around or become a damn heroin addict, but I never for one friggin' moment gave up on this one glorious life we've got to live!"

TO BOSTON AND THE COMBAT ZONE

"About two months after the operation, using the Jaguar my boss lent me, I started going back and forth between the two locations like before, doing pretty much what I had been doing before the accident, only on crutches. Seeing ol' Jakie boy on crutches but still working out like a fiend and doing everything he'd always done, and even more so, proved to be an inspiration to the people I was training, and a good ol' time was had by all.

"The two owners from Boston were extremely pleased with how things were going up in Maine, as you can imagine, and they began urging me to go down to Boston and manage a new fitness club they had just opened up in what was called 'The Combat Zone' which was a hard-core section of downtown Boston that was made up of Mafia-operated night-clubs, strip joints, and every other conceivable kind of morally corrupt and illegal activity. Just my kind of scene!

"Ever since I arrived back in Portland from the West Coast, people had been talking to me about the Combat Zone, but I had never been there. I guess with managing the health clubs, then dealing with my leg, going down to Boston just didn't happen. I've always tended to walk into the jaws of the nearest beast, though, and the Combat Zone was sort of a natural next step for me. Hell, the name alone had me drooling to get there!

"Barbara had serious reservations about me moving to Boston and managing a health club in the middle of the Combat Zone so soon after my operation, but what could she do, look who she was dealing with. So she did the only thing she could do under the circumstances, which was to move to Boston with me. She, of course, never stepped foot in the vicinity of the Combat Zone in all the time we lived in Boston, though. She wasn't at all happy about me being in the center of all that sin and corruption, either. She had a very interesting and fulfilling life of her own on the other side of town as a very highly-paid private duty nurse for a very select clientele, so she led her life, and I led mine. We were together just about every night, though, and that meant a lot, know what I mean?"

"Yeah, I do," I said, without looking up from my notebook.

Ad featuring Jake, written and designed by him.

*His boss at Mid-City thought that "Jay"
sounded more classy than 'Jake'.*

Jake at Mid-City Health Club, displaying the crutches he was on when he moved from Maine to manage the club.

"The Portland and Lewiston clubs were fun, but when I landed in the Combat Zone I felt like I had been called up to the Major Leagues. The Combat Zone was where the famous, the infamous, and all those in between, went to misbehave in many different and exciting ways, and there I was, holding court, right in the middle of it all. The health club I managed was named the Mid-City Health Club, and it was on the corner of Washington and Beach Streets, directly across the street from The Intermission Lounge, which was the biggest, baddest bar in the Combat Zone. If it was bad, somebody could make money at it, and if you had said money, you could find it there, be it any kind of sex, drugs, or whatever. The wild-assed fun and craziness just kept coming, twenty-four hours a day. The Combat Zone was so thick with prostitutes of every shape, size, color and gender that they'd rush your car in a group when you were stopped at a red light, whether your wife or girlfriend was with you or not. Hey, maybe she wants some action too, they figured, otherwise why would she even be here?

"I've always been very history conscious, of course, so I thought of the Combat Zone as being a poor man's garden of pleasures in the middle of Brahmin Boston, and very much in keeping with the egalitarian principles that this great country was founded on. The working class has to have its fun too, you know? That's not to say that we didn't have a few Brahmins come into the Mid-City Health Club, though. We had members from every walk of life, from Harvard and M.I.T professors, to Mafia bosses, to over-educated street sweepers. I treated them all the same, regardless of pedigree or pocketbook, and that created an atmosphere that was very conducive to camaraderie among my clientele.

"Mid-City Health Club got to be the fashionable place to be seen. Newly-liberated uptown professional women liked to be seen in the window lifting weights – and they kept coming and coming, as long as we met them at their cars and walked them to the club and back. Some of them would scoot a little ahead now and then, so they'd be taken for a hooker, you know, just for the thrill of it. Humans are a very strange species, my friend. Anyway, what a scene we had going, with me as the ringmaster!

"We had this one Boston Blackie kind of guy, named Deluca, who used to come into the club pretty regularly, usually about every other day, but he never exercised or worked out in any way. Deluca would come in wearing casual street clothes, carrying a small gym bag in one hand, and carrying an expensive-looking new three-piece suit on a hanger in the other. A brand new three-piece suit, about every other day!

"When he first arrived he'd put the gym bag and suit in his locker in the shower room, then come back out and joke around with everybody for a while, telling stories that got everybody laughing, that kind of thing. Then after a while he'd go into the shower room and shave and shower, then he'd come back out a little while later dressed in his new three-piece suit, looking all clean and refreshed. That was his routine every friggin' time, man! And no one ever commented on it! No one asked him any questions. That was the Combat Zone for you!

"Turns out that Deluca was a master car thief who, for whatever reason he had, was only interested in stealing late-model Corvette convertibles. Must have stemmed from something he experienced in his childhood, I don't know. What he'd do is go to a Chevy dealership freshly showered and wearing that day's new three-piece suit, and ask to take a test drive in a Corvette. They'd accommodate him because of the grand impression he made, being so friendly, telling stories and everything, and looking so sparkly clean and well-dressed, then they'd never see him or the car again!

"I myself got somewhat involved in moving Deluca's stolen vehicles on the black market. On the off-days when he didn't come into the club, I'd hear a happy 'toot toot' and I'd look up and there he'd be, all smiles, driving by in a late-model Corvette, smoking a big cigar and giving me a happy little wave!"

JAKE

THE LACONIA, NEW HAMPSHIRE, BIKER RALLY

"My life wasn't all about the Combat Zone at that time, though. I was still big into motorcycles and really enjoyed blasting up the turnpike to Portland on a pretty regular basis. Maybe the fact that I had a steady supply of late model high-end motorcycles was a factor in my activities, I don't know. I've told you that some of my clientele at the club were professors from Harvard and MIT. Well, sometimes I'd be invited to one campus or the other to engage in some informal discussions with the professors and students on various subjects of interest to them. They seemed to enjoy the real-world perspective I had on some of the social issues of the time. In any event, I became quite interested in the motorcycles I spotted in the parking lots of those esteemed institutions, so I acquired an innocent-looking, one-ton ex-mail truck and would pull into one of the lots at four or so in the morning and load up. Not too many guys can dead-lift a 400-pound BMW motorcycle, you know. Add to it that I was still on crutches and you've got the picture. Hey, I figured I might as well make some practical use of all that muscle I put on by working out so hard. Once I had the bikes loaded onto the truck it was a cakewalk from there on. I became very good at chiseling identification numbers off motorcycle engines, turning ones into fours, threes into eights, and sevens into ones.

"I'd been a big fan of motorcycles since my teens, of course, but lately I'd been hearing about the existence of high-spirited, living outside the boundaries motorcycle lovers like myself forming what they were calling outlaw-biker clubs, and I was intrigued. So, about a year and a half after my motorcycle accident, I got my right leg up high enough to swing it over my Harley, after a few painful attempts, and made the trip to Laconia, New Hampshire, to attend the infamous 1965 national motorcycle riders rally at Weirs Beach, just for the hell of it."

"Oh! I remember that!" I said. "The Hell's Angels tore up the town! Everybody was very worried about it because we thought the Hell's Angels were way out in California, now there they were, terrorizing people in New Hampshire!"

"You, sir, have the story entirely wrong! If you have the friggin' time, sir, I will set you straight about a little bit of American history right now!"

I just looked over at him wide-eyed and listened.

"The Hell's Angels were falsely and maliciously accused of inciting and taking part in what became known as the Weirs Beach Riots," he began. "The true story is that some other unruly outlaw-bikers tore up the town so bad that the National Guard was called in, and the biased and unfair media decided that the Hell's Angels were the chief instigators and perpetrators behind it. That was later proven to be absolute bullshit, but there you go."

"Okay, Jake," I said. "It means a lot to me to know that, but mostly I'm interested in talking about how you first came into contact with the Hell's Angels in Laconia."

"What?!" he exploded. "Have I told you anywhere along the line that I first met the Hell's Angels in friggin' Laconia, New Hampshire?!"

"I, ah, ah," I said.

"Okay, then, I shall proceed, if you don't mind. For your information, I did not meet up with my Hell's Angels brothers in Laconia, to my great regret. It just didn't happen. I had heard a lot of extremely interesting things about them, you know, from a guy at a gas station babbling about how cool the Hell's Angels were, and what fantastic, custom-made motorcycles they had, and when I heard the very attractive waitress at a diner I stopped at talking about them like she was going to cream in her jeans, I got even more interested.

"And lo and behold, there was a full-page story about the riots and the Hell's Angels alleged part in them in the *Laconia Express* newspaper I had picked up to read over lunch. It looked like all systems were go for me with the waitress, if I was interested, but after she left with my order I started reading the story, and by the time she came back with my food I had lost all interest in eating and had forgotten the attractive waitress even existed.

"The newspaper story made the Hell's Angels out to be such dirty, low-down, savage creatures that I thought surely such wonderful people could not exist! They were motorcycle-loving, thrill seeking, law breaking scourges upon society! Lovers of violence! An on-going threat to the sanctity of womanhood! The outlaws of the Wild West ride again! Just the band of men I had been looking for all of my life! These guys sounded too good to be true!

"But when the writer got into the loyalty and brotherhood the Hell's Angels felt for one another, I was hooked for good. That's what did it. The straight world might see it as adolescent gang-mentality carried to its worst extreme, but for me the absolute bond that seemed to exist between members of the Hell's Angels was the ultimate draw. I really didn't know it at the time, but I had been looking for my true family my whole life. That's what had been eating at me all those years. When I first heard of the Hell's Angels and what they were like and how they felt about each other, something down deep inside told me that my life would never be the same.

"And there on my wall is that very newspaper story, sir!" he yelled, jumping up from his chair and pointing over my head at a well-framed, very yellowed, full page newspaper story up on the wall across the room behind me.

"I've had that newspaper story about the Hell's Angels either up on the wall of every place I've lived in, or in an inmate property storage unit at some house of incarceration or another. It is therefore accurate to say that that newspaper story you see right there has been in my possession since the time I read it that day in Laconia, New Hampshire. It's the most important document in my life. I wouldn't part with it for the world. It is my Magna Carta, so to speak. Reading that newspaper story made me aware of what was missing in my life. When I became aware of the Hell's Angels and what they were about, I felt complete, and I was set free to fully appreciate this great and glorious life we've been given!"

And all this time I thought being an outlaw-biker didn't mean anything more than hanging out with a bunch of other guys who like to ride motorcycles as part of a group, drinking beer, and getting into all kinds of trouble with the law, just for the fun of it.

JAKE BY A NOSE

"I thoroughly enjoyed my visit to Laconia, especially reading about the Hell's Angels in the newspaper, but after a while it was time to say goodbye to the town and get back to Boston. It's that little bit of extra fun you hang around for that gets you in trouble, you know. The main reason I decided to leave, though, was because I didn't want the Hell's Angels to get the impression that I was chasing after them, for reasons that I've already told you.

"So, there I was, kind of proud of myself for not getting into any trouble on my little visit, headed out of town back to Boston, when big trouble just jumped right out in front of me. Wouldn't you know it, after all my good intentions.

"Out of nowhere, I found myself involved in a very unfriendly encounter with a big, beefy, sweaty outlaw-biker with a very antagonistic attitude. His girlfriend and I locked eyes as I was cruising by a bunch of local bikers and their women parked along the roadside, and after I pulled over to chat with her, he came out of nowhere and was immediately in my face with his beer breath and fucking frothy mouth, yelling his ugly-ass head off about what he was about to do to me. A big, fat, sloppy grunt hog like him wouldn't even have dared to come within striking range of me in normal times, but when he saw my crutches on the rack I had made for them on the back of my bike, he thought he could bully me, and you know how much I friggin' hate bullies.

"I knew right from the gitgo that this was a kill or be killed situation and my warrior survival instincts kicked in big time. He was standing, I was sitting, and there was no way for me to quickly jump off my bike with my right leg in the condition it was. Besides that, he outweighed me by at least a hundred pounds, and the mean sneer on his face made it very obvious that he was getting ready to lunge forward and pound the fucking shit out of me.

"There wasn't going to be any negotiating done, I knew that for damn sure, so I immediately catapulted into action!" Jake yelled, jumping up from his chair and crouching down as if he were straddling a motorcycle.

"My instincts and usual custom in a fight is to assume the role of aggressor, because it is generally better to hit than to be hit, but he was too close for me to get much into a punch with either of my hands, or to kick him with my left leg, so I did the only thing I could do to save my life! I fucking screamed like a wild banshee out of hell and lunged my head forward and clamped my teeth onto his fucking nose! I had a helluva chunk of it in my mouth and I twisted and yanked at it like a fucking wild animal until it came loose! Then I swallowed the fucking thing! I didn't mean to, it just kind of slid down my throat in the rush of things, but there you go, I swallowed the fucking thing!

"Biting off part of his nose proved to be quite effective as a defensive maneuver, as you might imagine," he continued, swinging his leg off the imaginary bike. "I have found over the years that taking the initiative in a confrontation is most often the best defense," he said matter-of-factly, sitting back down in his chair.

"The guy immediately began screaming in horror, and because blood was gushing out of the end of his nose onto my very cool leather jacket, I revved up my bike and casually cruised away. I never did find out how it all turned out until I ran into an outlaw-biker from Laconia in a bar a few years later who told me that the guy lived through it, and had had his nose reconstructed. He also told me that the story about me biting off a guy's nose and swallowing it at the Laconia, New Hampshire, motorcycle-rider rally had become legendary in outlaw-biker bars everywhere.

"Evidently, they took the meat to reconstruct the guy's nose from his ass, and the reconstructed part of his nose doesn't tan in the same way that the rest of his nose does, so it stands right out! He also told me that whenever local outlaw-bikers get together, they talk about the guy from Laconia who scratches his nose when his ass itches!"

"That'll give me one to chew on on my way home, Jake!" I said, laughing as I closed my notebook. "See ya next time! That's when you're going to tell me about how you first met the Hell's Angels, right Jake?! Right Jake?!"

"You got it!" he roared, thrusting his fist into the air. "Hell's Angels Forever!"

SEVEN

We usually met in Jake's apartment because we're both comfortable there – except for your Aunt Clara, Jake Sawyer is the best housekeeper in the world – and the small museum's worth of photos and memorabilia all over the walls and in every nook and cranny make for the ideal setting for our talks, but this time I really wanted to meet at a bar. Somehow or other, I couldn't pass on the experience of sitting at a bar with Jake Sawyer and having him tell me about how he first met up with the Hell's Angels. Jake didn't think much of meeting at a bar at first, because he's long since grown tired of the attention he gets when he walks through the door, he said, but after we batted it around a bit we agreed to meet at the Munjoy Hill Tavern, which is known for having that "Portland feeling" about it, and features prominently in local lore. When I suggested to Jake that the Munjoy Hill Tavern might be an appropriate place for the first Hell's Angel from Maine to talk about how he first met up with his Hell's Angels brothers, I knew I had him.

So there we were one afternoon, sitting at a table out in the backyard of the Munjoy Hill Tavern, just two guys having a beer and admiring the large mural on the outside wall of the tavern depicting scenes from Portland's history. Johnny Cash was singing *"San Quentin, I hate every inch'a you..."* on the jukebox inside, believe it or not, and we chuckled at the appropriateness of the background music. When I asked Jake if he thought one of the guys inside might have played the song in his honor, he snorted with derision and said he didn't give a shit either way. Such is celebrity.

"The Munjoy Hill Tavern holds a special place in Portland history," Jake began, "and I'm happy to be here to talk about the subject that we are going to talk about today, but the reaction of guys like that to seeing me walk through the door is the reason why I don't generally like going to public drinking establishments," he said, obviously going under the assumption that the song was played for him.

"I've done a lot of wild and crazy things in this town, and I've made a big impression on a lot of people, both for good and bad, and the beat goes on. There's too many guys in bars who treat me with a kind of awe, and I know they're shaking in their boots when they're talking to me. It gets old. They always want to talk about this and that thing they've heard I've done, but they've got the story so garbled up that it's not worth my time to set them straight, and they wouldn't understand anyway.

"True and entirely accurate stories are hard to find even in a friendly neighborhood tavern like this one, or just about anywhere else, for that matter, my friend," he continued, "but that's what you're going to get from me today. We're going to be talking about the most important event of my life, which is, of course, how I met up with my Hell's Angels brothers and realized my destiny! And you're going to get all the gory details right from the mouth of the horse's ass that lived through it all!

"Hell's Angels Forever!" he roared, thrusting his clenched fist into the air.

Right away two guys inside started yelling, "Hell's Angels Forever!" and "Yea Jake! Yea Jake!" and I could see what he meant about the adulation stuff. He tried waving it off, like who cares, but I detected a little smile.

JAKE

Animal and Tiny, cruising through Oakland.

The levity didn't last long, though. He became very serious and sat ram-rod straight, with his shoulders squared off, looking over at me with a stern look on his face. I got that little quiver in my stomach I hated myself for, but I tried my damnedest not to let it show. Damn, I thought I was all through with that stuff.

"Before we get started, sir," he said, "we need to address some concerns I've had lately, and I have decided that those concerns would be best addressed by having a statement I wrote out last night printed word for word in any publication my remarks might appear in," he continued, repeating the 'word for word' with a squint-eyed look over to me. Reaching into his watch pocket and pulling out a small, neatly folded piece of paper, calmly and methodically unfolding it, he began reading from it, barking each word distinctly, giving each syllable its proper due and emphasis, with me acting as his dutiful stenographer:

"I, Jonathan 'Jake' Sawyer, hereby unequivocally state that I have no knowledge whatsoever concerning any of my Hell's Angels brothers, or anyone in any way associated with the Hell's Angels Motorcycle Club, as ever having broken any law, or laws, of any kind, in any way, at any time, and anyone who construes in any way that I do have such knowledge, and acts in any way whatsoever on their misconceptions, does so at their own discretion, and at their own immediate peril."

So be it noted.

"I don't want to come off as a paranoid wacko, my friend," he said, obviously relieved to be done with the matter, "but as long as the arm of the law is, there are arms that are longer, if you know what I'm getting at ..."

All I knew at that point was that Jake was the first Hell's Angel from Maine, and that he had become a member of the club in the tumultuous 1960s when California was the happening place and the Hell's Angels had become counter-culture heroes whose brutally violent and outrageously hedonistic behavior was sure to have come to Jake's attention. I assumed that he had immediately rushed off to Oakland, California, in a fit of passion to join up with the Hell's Angels in the same way that John Ford, the six-time Academy Award winning movie director from Port-land, had rushed off to Hollywood to make films about fifty years earlier.

"Well, no, that wasn't quite the case," he said when I asked him about him and John Ford. "But close, I guess, now that I think of it," he laughed, "we're talking hot 'en heavy heated passion in both cases, for sure. Making movies was on John Ford's mind non-stop as soon as he saw his first flick, and the Hell's Angels were on my mind and in my heart from the moment I read the newspaper story about them I've got framed and hanging on the wall of my apartment. So there you go, maybe John Ford and I had something in common, after all."

I thought he'd see it that way after a bit.

"As we discussed the last time we spoke," Jake continued, "I did not happen to have any contact with any Hell's Angels in Laconia, but there was something about the way people talked about them that rang my chimes, big time. Everyone I came into contact with referred to them with a kind of awe and respect in their voices that I'd never heard before, and there was a hunger inside me to have people talk about me in that same way.

"After I got back from Laconia, Barbara said she saw something in my eyes that hadn't been there before, and at first she thought it was a woman I had met in Laconia, but when she found the *Laconia Express* story in my dresser drawer, she knew immediately that it wasn't a woman I was thinking about, it was the Hell's Angels. She also knew that I was going to be traveling to wherever I had to go to be with them, with or without her. Hey, I hadn't even thought it through that far myself, but she saw it all in a flash.

"Added to that situation was that I was starting to lose my liking for the Combat Zone scene. The last time you and I talked we got into my exciting adventures as a fitness trainer to Boston blue bloods and underworld figures, and all the wild crazy-assed shit I was involved in, but we didn't get into the downside of it all. It was fun, sure, but after a while it became quite hazardous, man. I was delivering late-model stolen automobiles and BMWs to people who lived in swanky neighborhoods on almost a weekly basis, so that meant that a lot of high-placed people had had their car stolen, ya know? I was into a lot of other risky shit with some very undesirable and violent people. A lot of 'pay up or else you'll keep seeing me' kind of jobs, that sort of thing. I was also consorting with pimps and whores on a fairly regular basis and sharing in the profits to be made. I was making a whole lot of money, no question, but it wasn't money I was after. Making money has never been my object in anything I've done in my life. As I have said before, it was the fascination I had for the action itself. I just couldn't say no to any of it, and the heat was all around me. No one lasts long in the underworld. Either I was going to be grabbed by the back of the neck by law enforcement and be carted off to a cold, dark cell sometime soon, or some under-world nobody who didn't think he got his proper cut of my last piece of action was going to be waiting for me around the corner some night with a dumb smile on his face and a snub-nosed revolver in his hand.

"Barbara picked up on the state of affairs before too long, of course, and became intent on getting me out of the Combat Zone while I still had my health and all my body parts, especially my right leg, she said, because she'd seen what I'd gone through to save it. She had become a highly sought-after private duty nurse during the time we'd been in Boston, so she could pretty much choose where she wanted to live, and I was always raving to her about how fabulous California was when I lived there before, so here we go. She gets on the situation big time and lands a position as a private duty nurse for Henry J. Kaiser, of Kaiser Steel and Aluminum, who lived in a penthouse in Oakland, California which, of course, is where the home base of the Hell's Angels happened to be located!

"She didn't say anything to me about my going to Oakland to meet the Hell's Angels, though, because she knew I wouldn't drag her all the way out to California for just that alone. Instead, she went on and on about me going to Oakland and opening up a chain of 'Jake Sawyer Health and Physical Fitness Salons' all up and down the California coast. Fortunately, I had enough ill-gotten money to make that happen so, before very long, we both said our goodbyes around Boston, and there we were, out on the open highway in my stolen black Corvette convertible, pulling my stolen late-model BSA motorcycle behind us in a trailer, barreling like hell across America, laughing our asses off all the way!

"We'd get off the highway now and then and hop on that BSA and take life-threatening rides up the sides of mountains and down country roads that go on forever! Barbara's long blonde hair would be flying straight back, and I'd be howling my fucking head off just for the pure joy of it! We loved each other and we loved the people we met along the way! America is a great country! I could tell you stories, man! High adventures! Sex! Drugs! Violence! Stories that will break your heart! Stories that will make you laugh your ass off! Whatever you want!"

"Some other time," I said without looking up from my notebook, "let's get to the Hell's Angels."

*Fu Man Chu, president of the Fresno chapter of the
Hell's Angels in the 1960s.*

BACK TO CALIFORNIA

"So, there we were in California in the year 1965!" he
said excitedly. "Right smack in the middle of the
mystical, magical 1960s! Man, it was like walking into
another world! There was a feeling in the air that
nobody had ever experienced! Peace and love,
psychedelics, hip-pies, long hair on men, women with

their nipples showing through very flimsy t-shirts, wild-assed anti-war protests in the streets, all with the pungent smell of pot in the air! The place was even more exciting than when I was there before! We were a long way from the Combat Zone in more ways than one, my friend!

"Barbara was literally on top of the world. Henry J. Kaiser lived in a penthouse apartment on the top floor of Kaiser Center, which is the tallest building in Oakland and overlooks Lake Merit and Lake Merit Park. She spent a lot of time in his penthouse with him, and she and Mr. Kaiser became very close. Hey, she liked and respected him, he was very generous with her, she had a great view, and, ah, so did he. So there you go!

"I was spending part of my days scouting out locations for my first health club, mostly so I'd have something to tell Barbara about that night, but I think you know what I was really up to.

"It would have been a simple matter for me to find out where the Hell's Angels clubhouse was and just go there, but that's not the way it's done in the outlaw-biker world. It would be like showing up at a lady's doorstep before you'd been formally introduced to her, or something like that. It's just not done. Pull up on your bike at an outlaw-biker clubhouse where nobody knows you, and you'll most likely get beat to a bloody pulp and thrown into the nearest dumpster with your bike hoisted up and thrown in on top of you, after they'd stripped it of the parts they wanted, of course.

"I knew that most outlaw motorcycle clubs always have a bar in the area that they've taken over for their private and personal use, and I found from talking to a guy in a bar that the Hell's Angels had taken over a bar named the Luau Club, on East 14th Street, which was in a rundown section of Oakland. The guy who told me about the Luau Club also told me that I'd better stay the hell out of it if I wanted to stay alive for any length of time.

"He got all excited when I asked him about the Hell's Angels, actually. They were the hottest topic in Oakland, by far. Hell, they were the hottest topic in the entire country. When he said 'Luau Club' he raised his voice so everybody at the bar could hear him, and they all crowded around us and backed him up about the place totally, one-hundred percent. Stay the fuck out of there, they all said. One guy plunked himself on the stool beside me and said I looked like a big strong guy who could take care of himself, but there were a few things I maybe ought to know if I was thinking of going to the Luau Club.

Lowell and Salem Hell's Angels in 1969. They were the first Hell's Angels on the east coast, and they were led by Donald "Skeets" Picard, back row (tall, handsome in a black t-shirt, and Hawkeye is to his left). Jake says he still loves them all!!!

JAKE

"The first thing I needed to know, he said, is that the Hell's Angels love to fight and they don't fight fair. One of them will pick a fight with you over fucking nothing, then the others will jump in while you're fighting him. You fight one of them, you fight them all. If I went to the Luau Club I'd be on my own, he said, no matter what happened, because the Oakland Police Department had a policy of not responding to calls made from the Luau Club, no matter what the call was about, or who was calling. He said what I was going to hear if I called them was: 'You went to the Luau Club knowing what was up, right? You can take care of your own ass now, sir. Bye now.'

"Man, the Luau Club sounded like such a fun place! I couldn't wait to get there!

"How it was all going to come down was the question, though. I took a long and leisurely motorcycle ride around San Francisco Bay, trying to decide. I considered a few options, but I couldn't land on anything that would give me that feeling of absolute confidence I knew I had to have. Later that night, at home, Barbara could see that something was going on with me and she was right on it.

"Out of nowhere, she did something that shocked the shit out of me, something that was completely unlike her. All of a sudden she jumped up out of her chair and ran across the room and screamed in my face: 'Get this goddamn thing settled! Go right for it and take whatever happens, either way! Be who you are! That's what you've always done, so do it now! Walk into that low-life dirty stinking place and tell those damn Hell's Angels that you're half in love with them and that you're there to find out if it's the real thing!'

"Man, that lady could tell it to me like nobody else has before or since."

THE LUAU CLUB

"After Barbara's little tirade, I realized that the only thing I could do was to be myself, and who I was at the time was a respected physical fitness trainer with a lot of flair, so that's the way I had to present myself. When I went to make the acquaintance of the Hell's Angels I had a James Dean haircut and I dressed the way I always dressed, which is described in the lyrics of my all-time favorite song, 'Black Denim Trousers,' which was recorded by Vaughn Monroe in 1955. Mr. Monroe is no longer with us, so I shall sing the chorus for you myself, my friend:

He wore black denim trousers and motorcycle boots,
And a black leather jacket with an eagle on the back,
He had a hopped up cycle that took off like a gun,
That fool was the terror of Highway 101.

Hey, wha' d'ya know, his singing voice isn't all that bad. Not all that good, either, actually, but, whatever.

"So, just like the song says," he resumed, "I went to the Luau Club wearing black denim jeans, highly polished motorcycle boots, and the very cool black leather jacket with an American eagle on the back that's hanging on my wall today! Yes, I still am in possession of that very jacket I wore that day, my friend! It has been prominently displayed on the wall of every place I've lived in over the past fifty-five years, including, of course, my present domicile! I've been offered very serious money for that jacket on many occasions over the years, but there is absolutely no way that I would ever part with it!

"When I pulled up across the street from the Luau Club in my stolen, absolutely dazzling, new black Corvette convertible, I could see a couple of guys staring out a small side window at me, trying to figure out what I was all about and what the hell I was doing in that part of town.

"The two guys disappeared from the window when I got out and started to cross the street, of course. Hell's Angels aren't gawkers, especially on their own turf. When I went through the door and looked around, I saw immediately that the place was as dingy and rundown as I had been told, and I knew for sure that the Luau Club was the Hell's Angels bar, alright.

"There were about a dozen guys around the room, all wearing faded, beat up denim vests with 'Hell's Angels' printed on the back across the top, and 'Oakland' at the bottom. Most of them were smoking cigarettes and drinking beer, of course, and none of them looked up when I came in. Some of them were sitting at tables together, a couple of them were at the pool table in the middle of the room shooting a game, and a few others were just milling around the room, singing along with the music on the jukebox.

"I remember very well what song was playing on the jute-box when I walked in. It was 'These Boots Are Made For Walking,' by Nancy Sinatra, and the guys up dancing and singing their heads off were yelling 'stomping!' in place of 'walking.' When they yelled 'stomping!' they'd crash their boots down on the floor so hard dust rose from the cracks and made it very hard to breathe.

"When I went over to the bar and ordered a beer the

bartender shot a quick glance over at a big guy with a thick beard and long black hair sitting at a table across the room, and when the guy looked over at me and gave me the up and down, then nodded his head to the bartender to give me a beer, I knew who was calling the shots in the place.

*Hell's Angels at the infamous
Luau Club in Oakland in 1966.*

"The one hook I had going for me was that I was buddies with a guy in the Combat Zone, named Arty Dorherty, who said he was a friend of a very prominent member of the Hell's Angels named Tiny. When I told Arty that I was going to Oakland to maybe meet up with the Hell's Angels, he gave me his telephone number and said to have Tiny give him a call, and he'd put in a good word for me. I had even called Arty earlier in the day to be sure he'd be around later to take what would be a very important telephone call from me. No matter who you are, or what you're like, you don't get anywhere with outlaw-bikers without a good personal reference. That's just the way it is, and if you try to go any other route your life won't be worth bird shit on the sidewalk on a rainy day.

"So after I got my beer, I walked over to the big guy in charge, and said, 'Hello, my name is Jake Sawyer. I'm from Portland, Maine, and I'm looking for a man named Tiny.'

"The guy I was talking to wasn't Sonny Barger, the legendary leader of the Hell's Angels, who I was very eager to meet; it was Terry the Tramp, I found out later. I also found out later that Terry was an exception to what Hell's Angels generally were like, just like I was. He came from a well-to-do family and was very well educated, and was also very healthy and physically fit looking. Terry and I were later to become good friends, but he wasn't very nice to the new kid on the block that day at the Luau Club.

"He didn't even look up at me when I asked him about Tiny, he just shot a quick look over at the guy sitting next to him, shrugged his shoulders, and said, 'Portland fucking Maine? What the fuck is that?' and every guy in the place laughed out loud like they had never heard anything so funny. Then after a while, with me just standing there wondering what the hell was going to come next, Terry yelled 'Tiny!' and this guy across the room, stands up and yells: 'What the fuck?!'

"So I walk over to the guy and tell him that Arty Dorherty from the Combat Zone says hello, and that he can call him and Arty will tell him all about me.

"Right away, Tiny sits down and says, 'I ain't calling fucking nobody! Why should I give a fuck who you are?!'

"While this was all going on, I could see that all the

other guys around the room were watching what was going on very intently. Whenever a stranger walks into an outlaw-biker bar, good times are usually right around the corner. A lot of guys think they can hang in with outlaw-bikers, buy them a few beers, shoot the shit a little, and right away, they're an old buddy. Not even close. The reason outlaw-bikers have their own bars is the same reason they ride customized-for-speed motorcycles and live like fucking savages. The only people we like and feel comfortable with are other outlaw-bikers. No matter how tough a guy is, or how much of a good guy he tries to be, he usually gets the living shit beat out of him at some point if he happens to wander into an outlaw-biker bar. Hell, outlaw-bikers like to fight so much they fight each other if there's no one else around, so why the hell wouldn't they beat up on a friggin' stranger?

"So here I was, walking into the Hell's Angels bar, freshly showered and clean shaven, making unreasonable demands on their brother Tiny. I could almost hear the wheels turning in their heads about bouncing me off the walls for a while, then taking possession of my new Corvette across the street, since after they got through with me I'd no longer have any use for it anyway.

"I couldn't get Tiny to get up off his fat ass to make the call to Arty, I knew that, and I sure as hell wasn't going to ask him again, so I got the bartender to put the phone on the bar and I made the call myself.

"As I stood there listening to Arty's phone ring and ring, I became very anxious thinking about what a crazy fuck he was and how fucking foolish I was to put my fate in his hands. He was the wildest, most crazy-assed biker in Boston, and I wasn't at all surprised that he was tight with one of the Hell's Angels. Arty had the first chopper in New England, as a matter of fact, and he loved to go out to Logan airport and race airplanes as they were taking off. He was in the Boston newspapers for it, and had become some kind of cult hero in the Combat Zone. That was great for him, I guess, but all he was for me that day in the Luau Club was a demented dude across the country who wasn't answering his telephone.

Photo taken by Jake of some of his Hell's Angels brothers stopped at a gas station on the way to the Hell's Angels annual blow-out in the hills of Cucamonga near Berdoo, California. Sonny Barger, the president of the club, is on the motorcycle to the left. Standing next to him, holding a can of beer, is Zorro, with his arm around his brother, Tiny.

"Then I hear his voice on the other end! Hallelujah! Right away he's all happy to hear from me and tells me to put Tiny on, no problem.

"I had to go through some shit to get Tiny to come over to the phone, of course. He was very comfortable where he was, and, like he said, what the fuck did he care one way or another who I was, but after I bought him and every guy in the place a beer, I managed to get him off his ass and over to the bar and on the phone with Arty.

"I was very relieved, but I was not at all prepared for what happened next.

"Arty told Tiny that I was a fucking asshole and that they had me chased out of the Combat Zone! He told them that every outlaw-biker in Boston had been screwed over by me in one way or another, and that my life wouldn't be worth a pile of duck shit if I ever returned to anywhere near the East Coast!

"Tiny looked over at me with a very mean and menacing look in his eye, and he told Arty that if there was anything left of me after they got through with me they'd mail my fucking remains back to fucking Boston for them to mix with their fucking baked beans. Everybody in the bar started hooting and howling their friggin' heads off when he came out with that one, but I wasn't too friggin' amused, especially after they started stomping on the floor again and grinning at me through the dust that came up through the cracks in the floor.

"Holy fuck! I knew that asshole Arty was just screwing around, because that's what the friggin' halfwits that hang around the Combat Zone do, everything's always a big damn hilarious joke with them, but this was no time for joking around!

"I grabbed the phone from Tiny and, sure enough,

I heard Arty on the other end laughing his damn ass off.

"I put the fear in him real quick, though. He knew what I was capable of, and when he heard how friggin' mad I was he started to get real sorry, real fast. I told him that if I lived through this I was going to be a passenger on the next fucking plane he raced at the airport, and when the plane stopped, I was going to step out of it and chase him the fuck down and break his fucking neck and cram his entire fucking customized chopper piece by piece up his lying friggin' ass, then I was going to throw him and his chopper out into the Charles River to see if shit really does float! He knew damn well I wasn't kidding, and he asked me to put Tiny back on the phone.

"After our little chat, Arty had a much different tune to sing to Tiny, you can be sure of that. It was all a big joke and I'm really a great guy, Arty told him. Now I was this big fucking macho hero who was everybody's friend to the end, and could do no wrong. Arty definitely didn't want to see me coming back to the Combat Zone, so he laid it on real thick. Tiny was looking over at me with, well, almost admiring eyes by the time Arty got through telling him about me. When he gave me back the phone, so I could say goodbye, though, I slammed the fucking thing down in Arty's ear, and I could tell by the look on Tiny's face that he admired that, and I knew we were going to be friends someday.

"Of course, when Tiny told the guys all the groovy things Arty said about me, I expected that they would hate my fucking guts even more than they would have otherwise, because now I was not only a very good-looking, stylishly-dressed, extremely well-built stud, who was driving a fancy car, I was also a hero of the friggin' Combat Zone underworld.

"That's the way it usually is with men, after all. Any man who tells you he doesn't resent the abilities and achievements of the man standing next to him is a friggin' liar. It's just the way most men are put together. I'd been dealing with male envy all of my life, believe me, and I never expect anything else.

"That wasn't the way with the Hell's Angels in the Luau Club that day, though. There was an integrity about them that really impressed me. They knew what kind of balls it took for a man to walk into their bar dressed the way I was, and they could see that I wasn't some kind of whacked-out pain freak or sexual deviant who didn't give a rat's ass if he got beat up or not. Outlaw-biker clubs get those now and then. No, I was completely fucking sane, and they could see that. I only acted insane, just like they did.

"After Tiny had told them what Arty said about me the guys left me alone at the bar for a while, because they were Hell's Angels, after all. They weren't about to gather around me like excited schoolgirls, that was for sure. After a little while, though, Terry the Tramp came over to me and we shot the shit about this and that a little, then he asked me if I'd ever done any arm-wrestling. That made me smile because I had been exceptionally good at arm wrestling from a very early age. I was a contestant in the East Coast Arm Wrestling Championships a few years after this time period, my friend, and finished runner-up to the eventual world champion two years in a row, even though I was the lightest man in the competition, but I will tell you more in detail about that when we reach that time period in my life. For the moment, though, let's just say that I was quite happy that Terry had brought up the subject of arm wrestling, and I, of course, told him that a friendly bout would be most welcome.

"So Terry and I walked over to the pool table, with all of the other guys following us, and plunked our elbows down on it across from each other, grabbed paws, and got ready to go at it. The way it's done is that another man puts his hands over both of yours, and when he lifts his hand, the bout begins."

At this point, Jake jumped up from our table at the Munjoy Hill Tavern and walked over to the table next to ours and plunked his right elbow down on it, as if it were the pool table at the Luau Club, and he was facing Terry the Tramp on the other side.

"As soon as our grips tightened, I knew Terry was no match for me," he said. "He was a strong guy, no question, but I'd beaten many men who were a lot stronger.

"My match with Terry did not last long. I could have beaten him sooner but I chose not to, for obvious reasons. He said I cheated, so we went at it again, and after I won again, he seemed to be satisfied.

"After I got to know him, I found out that Terry was a self-obsessed Adonis who hated losing, just like I do. Anyway, after I put his arm down he said I 'jumped,' which means that I threw my body weight into my arm, which you are not supposed to do. In a certified competition bout the put-down has to be 'clean,' meaning by arm power only.

"Terry didn't continue his little charade for long, though. He was actually a very mature individual, and it was as obvious to him as to everyone else in the bar that I had beaten him fair and square, so there was no need for us to go at it again. After a while, he sincerely asked me how I got to be so strong, so I told him my work-out routine, and he told me his.

Terry the Tramp

"Everything was kind of quiet for a while, like they were trying to get their heads around whatever it was that I was all about, then out of nowhere, somebody, I think it was Moldy Marvin, yelled: 'Who the fuck is this guy?!' and the way he said it, like he could hardly believe what he was witnessing, cracked all of us up big time.

"After that, things were different. Everybody got a lot looser and guys started coming over and asking me all about myself. There were a few things that had registered with them, after all. They heard me tell Arty

Dorherty over the phone exactly what I was going to do to him, and they realized that Arty knew beyond any doubt that I was serious, that I'd actually do it. They also knew I could have slacked off on beating Terry at arm wrestling as bad as I did, but I didn't, and when I beat him I could have been a hell of a lot more humble than I was, but I wasn't. I just fucking wasn't. Because I didn't want to be, that's all, and they respected the hell out of that. You have to know the breed.

"They were fascinated with me, to tell you the truth, and after a while I got into telling them numerous war stories about everything I had done. I didn't tell one fucking lie either. They just about fell on the floor laughing when I told them about how I got fired for what I did up on stage with the stripper at the county fair I took the General Motors execs to, but the story about me biting the guy's nose off in Laconia and swallowing it blew their fuckin' minds altogether!

"After all of this had transpired, I knew beyond any doubt that I wanted to become a member of the Hell's Angels Motorcycle Club. I wanted so bad to be a part of the brotherhood I witnessed that day that my head was buzzing at the thought of it.

"As time went on that day at the Luau club, though, I could sense that my little dog and pony show had gone on about long enough. Moods can shift very quickly in an outlaw-biker club. As soon as it occurred to me it might be time to leave, I left. I didn't go around trying to shake anyone's hand with a lot of happy to meet you, see you again, kind of bullshit thrown in, I just left. Social niceties aren't received well at outlaw-biker bars. Such a misstep at the end could have doomed me forever.

"I knew sure as hell I'd be back, though! The drive

home from the Luau Club will live in my mind forever, man! I was so empowered and bursting with confidence and joy I thought I was going to explode!"

EIGHT

Now that we had reached the point in our talks where Jake had met the Hell's Angels, I was eager to have him tell me about how he actually became a full-fledged member of the club, and what it was like hanging around with them on a daily basis. When I suggested to him that we meet at the Munjoy Hill Tavern again, he was immediately all for it.

"Sure!" he exclaimed, "what better place could there be to continue our little historical narrative! You're looking at the first Hell's Angel from Maine right here! In case you haven't taken it into account, I want to make note of the fact that Maine isn't exactly your leading motorcycle-riding state. The winter lasts a long time up here. There's snow and ice all over the roads for a good part of the year. Riding motorcycles in Maine is a little like snowshoeing in Florida, you know?"

In any event, there we were again the next afternoon, out in the backyard of the Munjoy Hill Tavern, seated at the same table as before. This time we had the whole place to ourselves, though. A slow afternoon, the waitress inside told us.

"So, Jake," I began, "it sounds like your first meet-up with the Hell's Angels went very well, indeed. At least they didn't chop you up into little pieces and throw your body parts into the dumpster across the street, huh?"

"Yeah," he answered, "and I was thankful for that. Hey, it could've happened even after we hit it off so well, just because it occurred to one of them to do it. One has to be extremely cautious about not taking anything for granted with outlaw bikers, after all.

Especially he Hell's Angels, who are very quick to pick up on a presumptive attitude.

"I knew that I hadn't been accepted by them just because I provided them with some entertainment one afternoon, but I also knew that my life would never be the same after I met them, so I decided to just go for it. I dropped the charade of looking for a location of what was supposed to be the first one of a string of 'Jake's Sawyer Health and Fitness Salons' up and down the California coast, and I became a regular at the Luau Club. My routine was to work out very vigorously in the morning, as has been my life-long habit whenever circumstances allowed, then I'd throw my leg over the Harley I had bought from my Hell's Angel brother Skip and be at the Luau Club by noon. Skip was from Massachusetts and was in the Navy, stationed in Oakland before he was discharged and joined the club. He was very smart and damn tough, and he gave me a lot of good advice that helped me fit into the club and grow as a man. Anyway, I was very happy just to hang around with the Hell's Angels doing whatever, but if I got a chance to go on a ride with them, I jumped on it every time and I'd stay with them for however long I could, no questions asked.

"I have described for you the feeling of riding a customized-for-speed motorcycle doing ninety-miles per hour through heavy traffic on a busy California freeway in the company of the Hell's Angels, have I not? It's the most thrilling and transporting ex-perience I have ever had in my life, and you're talking to someone who has jumped out of airplanes, rap-pelled down mountains, and done every crazy and extremely dangerous thing that was ever put in front of him to do!

"Being with the Hell's Angels was a lot more than

just riding motorcycles, though. For the first time in my life I was with men who I could totally trust and respect. We looked each other square in the eye and told each other the truth, every time. No pretense whatsoever. I had never felt more free to be myself, yet I had never felt more connected to the people around me. When I was with the Hell's Angels I felt incredibly grounded, as if life finally had some meaning, yet at the same time I felt levitated, like I was walking on air and my world was expanding. I was smitten, I guess. Yes! That's it! I was in love!

"The Hell's Angels were shaking their heads about me, though. You have to understand that I was a real oddball to them. Most of them didn't change their clothes for weeks, and almost never took a bath, but I showered and wore clean clothes every day. Hey, I'd show up after working out all morning and drink a quart of milk in front of them. I also didn't smoke cigarettes, get drunk too often, or gulp handfuls of pills. Well, not on a regular basis, anyway. I did do a little tripping now and then, you know, what with Timothy Leary and Ken Kesey being friends of the Hell's Angels and living not too far away. But, all in all, I guess I did do a lot more than I want to let on to, but you get my drift.

"I didn't stop being weird just because some of them made fun of me for it, though, and they respected me for that. I amused the hell out of them. I was what outlaw-bikers call a 'hang-around.' I hadn't even become a 'prospect' for membership yet, but I didn't grovel at their feet like other hang-arounds did. I just kind of skated for being as weird as I was and sticking to it, I guess. I was an honorably discharged U.S. Paratrooper, a former Kentucky rum runner, and I knew everything there is to know about the maintenance and operation of Harley motorcycles, so that all helped. And, oh, it didn't hurt that I was as strong as an ox and absolutely loved fighting.

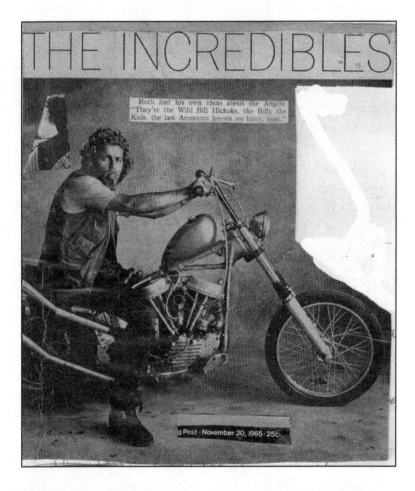

Ed Roth, California Hot-rodding superstar, had great insight to what the Hell's Angels are all about. "They're the Wild Bill Hickoks, the Billy the Kids, the last American heroes we have, man," he said. This photo appeared in the Saturday Evening Post, November 1965

JAKE

From left: Dirty Delbert, Slave Louie, Terry the Tramp, Free Wheelin' Frank and, seated at right, Blind Bob and Super Sharon. "She still rides with the club today, sixty years later!" Jake says.

"The Hell's Angels admire power and strength of any kind, no matter where they see it, and I had been lifting weights for many years and was a six-foot-two powerhouse. They'd seen puffed-up weightlifters like me before, though. Now and then one of those types would come into the Luau Club feeling their oats, but by the end of the evening they'd get beat up so bad they were lucky if they could crawl out the door. I didn't carry myself like some dumb-assed gorilla, though. If you hang with any outlaw-biker club for any length of time, you will definitely be involved in physical combat on a fairly regular basis. So they had seen me fight on a few occasions and realized that I was very light on my feet, extremely agile, and very fast, which is often more important than brute strength in fighting. You will remember that I was a starter in three varsity sports in high school and was known for my agility and quick movements. My Hell's Angels brothers said I was a white Muhammad Ali because of the way I danced around and hit with power. I was very pleased by that because Ali has always been one of my biggest heroes. He took on the world and won and was absolutely true to himself and everybody he met along the way. The man had a good mother, just like I did, and that's just about all you need in this life.

"Anyway, the Hell's Angels might have compared me to Ali, but that didn't mean that they were intimidated by my toughness in any way. Every one of them was damn tough himself, and loved fighting as much as I did.

"If you want to understand how powerful my attraction to the Hell's Angels was, consider that I had all of sunny California and everything it had to offer to choose from. I could have had any lifestyle I wanted. I could have associated with anyone, and done anything I wanted to do, but I chose to hang out at a run-down bar on East 14th Street, where I'd maybe get a chance to ride with a band of unruly outlaw-bikers now and then.

"I really didn't make a conscious decision to hang around the Hell's Angels, really, it was something that took me over. When I was with my Hell's Angels brothers I felt like I was with the family I had been looking for all of my life. Being with them was exactly like I knew it would be when I first read about them in that Laconia, New Hampshire, newspaper story that I've got up on my wall. I was head over heels in love with the Hell's Angels and the way they lived and related to one another from the moment I knew of their existence."

This shot of Jake straddling his Harley, wearing his Hell's Angels "colors", is prominent among the pictures and memorabilia-filled walls of Jake's apartment today.

VOLUME ONE

JAKE HUNG WITH BOB DYLAN!

"My big break came when I became the bartender at the Luau Club, which was not all that long after I first stepped into the place. Being given the bartending job was very significant, my friend, because it meant that I had made an extremely good impression on them. The bartender in an outlaw-biker club is a very central figure.

"Something that needs to be understood here is that the Hell's Angels had become national celebrities at just about the time I showed up. The news media couldn't get enough of them and women were hitchhiking across the country just to fuck Hell's Angels. They came into the Luau Club looking for Sonny, but he was almost never there, and we were only too happy to step in for him. I figured out later that he was home a lot figuring out how to create Hell's Angels chapters all over the world! He did it, too!! The sun never sets on the Hell's Angels!

"Anyway, we'd take the women in the back room and gang bang the hell out of 'em. They loved it. After we got tired of screwing them we'd get them drunk, throw them on the suicide seats of our bikes and take them to get 'Property of Hell's Angels' tattooed across the left cheek of their ass. There's a lot of older women out there today who have been sitting on that little memory for over fifty years, and lovin' every minute of it!

"We also had a lot of celebrities wanting to hang around us. In my first few weeks of hanging with the Hell's Angels I became acquainted with Bob Dylan, Neal Cassidy, Allen Ginsberg, and a bunch of other hot-shots in the arts and entertainment world. Terry the Tramp was banging Janis Joplin for quite a while. They say "Cry Baby" was written for him, and I wouldn't doubt it because she was absolutely in love with him. Terry was a big slut who was more interested in screwing camp followers than he was in having any kind of actual relationship, though, and he treated Janis just like she was another camp follower. She was typical of the celebrities who hung around us. They couldn't get enough of us, no matter how badly we treated them. I think it's that the Hell's Angels were real, you know, and the celebrities were living in un-real worlds, so we were like a salve to them. It's hard sometimes to deal with being famous, and I think they were so sick of having everyone around them kissing their asses all the time that it was good to have someone treat them like shit. All I know is that the more we made fun of them and otherwise abused them, the more they tried to impress us."

Wait a second, here. Did Jake just say he knew Bob Dylan? Bob Dylan? Trying to be casual about it, I asked him how much he remembered about him.

"He used to come in and sit at the bar sometimes when I was the bartender," Jake responded. "He never tried to impress anybody with who he was, ever. He was Bob Dylan, and that was that. I got to know him a little. We liked each other because we were a lot alike in many respects."

He let that remark hang in the air for a moment, then added, "But you knew I was going to say that, right?" he said, pointing at me and laughing.

"I didn't doubt it for a second," I said, grinning and keeping myself to my work.

"Hey, if you ever get tired of this bragging shit, just say so and I'll back off a bit," he said. "The only thing I can tell you, though, is that everything I'm telling you is true. Is it bragging if it's true? That's the kind of thing Dylan and I would get into now and then, actually. Hey, I'm not saying I was a friggin' guru to the guy or anything, but I was his bartender, and well, you know how that goes.

"Okay, so here's this wide-eyed Jewish kid from Hibbing, Minnesota, walking into an outlaw-biker bar in a run down section of Oakland, California. It was a very Dylan thing to do, of course. He was known for having a fascination with the underworld. I remember very well his sitting at the bar in the Luau Club telling me all about his meeting the famous mobster, Joey Gallo, during his Greenwich Village days. In fact, the song "Joey", which was on Dylan's 1976 album, *Desire*, was all about Gallo's life and death. You know he was killed at Umberto's Clam House, in Little Italy, New York, on his birthday, April 7, 1972, right?"

"Nope," I said.

"Well, anyway," Jake continued, "Dylan felt kind of safe walking into the Luau Club because he was used to hanging around with outlaws. He had a self-assurance about him that you respected. He didn't go out of his way to get along with us, he was just there. Anything could have happened, though, cool guy or not, you never know. It was an outlaw-biker bar and crazy things happened. It helped, of course, that we loved his music and played it all the time, whether he was there or not.

"Actually, the most important reason that Dylan was safe coming to the Luau Club was that he was friends with Sonny Barger. That automatically made him off-limits to any kind of harassment. Every celebrity in the country wanted to hang with Sonny. He was a sort of anti-celebrity, though. And that's what attracted celebrities to him. What a crazy fucking world. Sonny was just being himself and didn't give half a fuck about what anyone thought about anything he did. He's a happy, friendly guy, though. He was friends with all the band members of the Grateful Dead and Jefferson Airplane. He'd call Jerry Garcia a big tub of lard with a beard, and Jerry would say that Sonny was nothing but a big-mouthed smelly biker, but it was obvious they liked and respected each other.

"Okay, so you want a true to life Bob Dylan story?"

"Ya, ya, Jake, ya I do," I said.

"Here ya go," he said, chuckling. "One night Dylan invited us all to a party at the Mark Hopkins Hotel, which is the fanciest hotel in San Francisco. The Grateful Dead and Jefferson Airplane were staying there, and after Dylan and Sonny introduced us all around everything was going very smoothly. All those in attendance were friends of friends, so we were on our best behavior.

"Then some guy who was wearing a fashionable light blue suit and was sitting on a couch entertaining a group of people with his wit, stopped talking and held his nose like he was smelling something real foul when a Hell's Angel walked behind him. Well, what with all the tittering that took place after the guy did that, my Hell's Angel brother felt his only recourse was to take out his weapon of war and piss all over the guy from behind. He hosed the guy pretty good before he even knew what was happening!

"The incident ended up in all the celebrity gossip tabloids and evidently the guy's career never quite recovered from it. Getting pissed on in public is very bad for your image, especially because the guy didn't dare to complain and just hopped up off the couch and scurried out the door. After that, people would just snicker when his name was brought up. No one ever gets anything from the Hell's Angels they don't deserve, but they sure as shit are gonna get it if they do deserve it.

"Dylan got a helluva kick out of the whole thing, and when the Hell's Angels were asked to leave the party by hotel management, he accompanied Terry and me on his fire-engine red, 500cc Triumph Tiger 100 motorcycle to a houseboat rented by some friends of his in Sausalito, where we had a very nice time. There were two very attractive women there when we arrived and they took Bob, Terry and me out to a very fashionable restaurant.

"Terry and I were laughing about the reception we might receive in such an establishment, but no fear, we were treated like we were Clark Gable and Rock Hudson. People just couldn't wait for us to be bad, so they'd have a story to tell. They kind of sat back smiling, waiting for something to happen. Terry and I weren't in the mood to be bad, though, because we were with Bob Dylan and the two very pleasant women, not to mention that we were eating top of the line cuisine, which didn't happen all that often with us.

"After we left the restaurant, Bob invited us to join him on a houseboat a friend of his had tied up to a dock in Sausalito, and, of course, the two women rode with Terry and me on our bikes. That terrifying but broadening experience had the effect it always had on women, and by the time we got to the houseboat the ladies were very eager to ravage our bodies. Being utterly dependent on a man in the midst of danger, especially a misbehaving man, seems to bring out the beast in a woman. I'm not really sure where Dylan disappeared to, but we didn't much care. His two lady friends took very, very good care of us in his absence, so we didn't feel slighted in the least.

"A couple of days after that pleasant evening, we decided to pay Dylan another visit, since the time we had spent with him before was so much fun. Terry and I had gotten the impression that the two women from before were bi-sexual, or at least bi-curious, and that intrigued us, so we decide to have our favorite camp follower, Mama Judy, accompany us, just to see what might happen.

"Mama Judy was one helluva fine woman and was very much loved by the Hell's Angels. We never got tired of having her around. She was a strikingly beautiful blonde, with legs that went on forever, but she was also extremely intelligent and witty. We'd have raunchy sex with her, then we'd all be laughing our asses off together. The other camp followers hated her, of course. She had hitchhiked from Louisiana to fuck Hell's Angels and that's sure as hell what she did – and it didn't matter whose boyfriend you were. Mama Judy was also very tough. She'd get as much pleasure out of beating up on one of the other women as she did out of fucking their boyfriend.

Terry and I were aware that bringing Mama Judy with us to the houseboat was a delicate matter. If we showed up with her looking like she always did, you know, like she'd just been ravished by a pack of outlaw-bikers, it would be a major turn-off to the other two women. So we grabbed hold of her, had her take a shower, threw her onto the back of my bike and took her to a high-end women's apparel store. She objected all over the place, but we stuffed some bills in her hand anyway and instructed her to come out of the store with a complete set of new clothes, from panties and bra, on out. The whole enchilada. We also brought her to a cosmetics shop and made her go in and buy some lipstick and nice perfume. Man, I have to say that I was kind of losing my taste for Mama Judy, but when I saw how good she looked cleaned up, I almost didn't care whether we hooked up with the other two women or not.

"We could have called Dylan to see if he was going to be on the houseboat, but that wasn't the way we went about things. Even a small display of good manners would've tarnished our image. So we just showed up on the dock where the houseboat was tied up and sat there revving up our engines, and it wasn't long before our two lady friends emerged from the house boat all excited and very happy to see us. They said Dylan wasn't around, but we could come in and wait for him if we liked. We liked! Right on! Here Terry and I come, with the now very fashionable looking Mama Judy right along with us.

"Let's keep in mind here that it was in the middle of the wild and crazy counterculture of the 1960s and we're on a houseboat where Bob Dylan partied. Let's just say that there was a very high degree of excitement in the air.

"After a while, it became apparent that the two ladies were becoming infatuated with Mama Judy. The three of them were giggling all over the place and fooling around on the couch, when, out of nowhere, Mama Judy somehow had a wardrobe malfunction, and one of her very pretty and very firm breasts loosed its bounds from the new lacy bra she had just purchased for the occasion. From that point things heated up very quickly, believe me.

"Never had a plan come together quite so well. Terry and I were quite delighted with ourselves. It wasn't long before I was standing on the couch completely naked

JAKE

Mama Judy, with her back to camera, was awarded her own "special colors" by the San Francisco chapter, for services rendered. Jake says he can't identify all the Hell's Angels in the picture, but says Big Al Perryman is second from the left, Chocolate George is to his left in the background, and "Frisco" Pete is second from the right. Jake took the picture.

A photo that appeared in the Nov. 25th, 1965 issue of the Saturday Evening Post magazine. Top to bottom, Chocolate George, Fu Man Chu, and Mama Judy.

with Mama Judy and one of the other women strategically placed in front of me. Terry was across the room holding the third women inverted up against the wall, with each of them giving in to their most basic carnal desires. Then, right at the height of all the debauchery, guess who appears?! We looked up and there he was, Mr. Dylan, with a band mate of his!

"'Just in time!' I yelled. 'Jump in!'

"Dylan was immediately white-faced. He wasn't happy, mad, or embarrassed – he was just dumbfounded. *You're not in Hibbing anymore, Bobby,* I was thinking.

"'Whoa-a-a!' Dylan yelled, 'See ya later! We're gonna go get something to drink!' and he and his buddy went to a nearby restaurant for drinks. The proceedings on the house boat continued with barely a slow down for a good long time after they left, of course.

"Dylan went on a national tour after that, so we didn't see him for a while, but one night months later he walked into the Luau Club and when he saw me he yelled: 'Whoa-a-a!' just like he did that day when he walked in on the sex scene, and it cracked both of us up. These American icons are not half bad when you get to know 'em."

LIFE AT HOME

"So life with the Hell's Angels was grand, but things were not going too well with Barbara on the home front. We had been together for almost four years, through the two-year recovery period after my motorcycle accident, and through all of that Combat Zone insanity, but after we hit California we started growing apart. Well, she was growing, maybe I was regressing, I don't know, but it wasn't a good situation.

"She didn't pull the screaming in my face scene this time, though. We talked it all out very calmly. She was getting more and more involved in the upper-strata social life in Oakland, mainly through the people she was meeting through Mr. Kaiser, and I was hanging with the Hell's Angels all day. That should tell you something.

"On the outside, it was the same scenario as when we lived in Boston, actually. She was prominent in the straight world, and I was entrenched in the underworld, but the difference was that I didn't love the Combat Zone like I loved being with the Hell's Angels, and she knew it. She saw it in me as soon as I walked through the door after I got back from the Luau Club that night that I first met them.

"I know how strange and far-out it sounds, but I literally found a new love when I found the Hell's Angels. They replaced Barbara in my life. I was more in love with the Hell's Angels than I was with her, and a fellow's life can be very dramatically affected by things he does in the name of love."

We'd been all alone in the backyard patio area of the Munjoy Hill Tavern until a guy walked onto the scene in a very unobtrusive manner, seeming to be very hesitant about interrupting us, but it was as if he couldn't help himself.

"Hey, how ya doin'?" I said. "This is Jake and I'm Cliff, and we're talking about Jake's life story."

Right away the guy's eyes got all big and round. "Ya, ya, of course," he said. "They told me what you guys were doing here and I just wanted to say hello and introduce myself. My name is Stan Dobson and I'm the owner. Please keep on with what you're doing, though. Everything's on the house as long as you're here! Can I get you anything to eat or drink?"

Both Jake and I shook our heads no, but said that we appreciated the offer, and as he was backing away, Stan said: "I just wanted to let you guys know how happy I am that you're meeting here. I love Portland history and I love that my place is going to be part of the Jake Sawyer story."

"Okay, Stan" Jake said, "thank you, and carry on!"

"Actually," Jake said when Stan was gone, "Stan has been one of my best friends for many years. It's just that he's extremely modest and never pushes himself onto people. He just didn't want you to think he was trying to impress you with what good friends he and I are. To tell you the truth, I love the guy and would walk through the fires of Hell for him."

A PROSPECT

"As time went on," Jake continued, after Stan disappeared inside the tavern, "I became more and more desirous of becoming a patch-holding Hell's Angel, which means that you are an official member and are now authorized to call other members 'brother,' because when you become a patch holder that is what you are to each other.

"One does not become a member of an outlaw-biker club just by being in their presence for a certain amount of time and making friends with them, though. Far from it. One goes from being a 'hang around,' to a 'prospect,' to being a 'patch-holder,' and the process doesn't take a predetermined length of

The Hayward chapter of the Hell's Angels riding to the funeral of a brother who had been killed in a knife fight.

time. Each step lasts for as long as the patch-holding club members want it to. Many prospects spend a great deal of time going through dangerous and extremely demeaning treatment and are still not accepted. It's serious stuff, man. Becoming a member of the Hell's Angels means that you've been accepted into a brotherhood that is the same as the one that existed between members of the Roman legions, and bands of Viking warriors, both of which I have chromosomal memories of, my friend. I have written proof that I am a direct descendant of Rollo, who was the supreme leader of Viking 'Beserkers.' Now I was knocking on the door of being admitted into the inner circle of the present day version of such men. Being in an outlaw-biker club, especially the Hell's Angels

Motorcycle Club, isn't just something you do, some role you're playing, it's something you are, right to the very core of your being!

"I became an official prospect in early March of 1966, when I was twenty-eight years old, and I expected that the harassment would start at that time, but it didn't, at least not to the degree that other prospects went through. Once in a while a patch-holder would tell me to pour his beer into his glass, little stuff like that, but there was never any effort to totally humiliate me, like there normally was with prospects. The reasons for that are complex, but it had something to do with the ways in which I had already proven myself to them, and also the fact that I had been a United States Army Airborne Para-trooper.

"They had kind of made the paratroopers out to be more than it was, really, but I didn't try to disabuse them of their beliefs. Paratrooper training was hard, yes, but the truth is that what a recruit went through to become a paratrooper was a lot less than what I had watched Hell's Angels prospects go through, and I was happy as hell that I wasn't being treated like they were.

"At least in the paratroopers there are official limits on how far the training personnel can go. The Hell's Angels knew no such limits, and there was no set time when it would end. They'd keep you as a prospect for as long as they felt like it, and it took only one patch-holding member to block your name from coming up for a vote. You could go through all this shit for two or three years and if one brother black-balled you, that was it, so you treated each one of them with great respect at all times.

"The process of becoming a member of the Hell's

Angels Motorcycle Club is very similar to that of entering a monastery and committing yourself to a lifetime in the service to the Lord. The outside world no longer has any meaning for you, and you joyfully accept any hardship or challenge that is presented to you in your new life. As I have related to you, the Hell's Angels regarded Sonny Barger as the Messiah and we were all his disciples."

This is a picture of Hell's Angels leaving Sonny Barger's house in East Oakland to attend the funeral of Jim "Mother" Miles in Sacramento after he was killed in a motorcycle accident in January, 1966. "There must have been 200 Hell's Angels, including me, at the funeral," Jake says, "and that was almost all the Hell's Angels in the world at the time. We broke speed limits on the way back to Oakland, of course, in honor of Mother Miles. We loved him a lot then, and we still love him today – and you can take that to the bank."

From left:, Big Al Perryman, Fat Freddie, Crazy Red, Dirty Delbert, Jake "Bonecrusher" Sawyer, and Terry the Tramp

THE SUICIDE CHARGE

"I shall now relate a series of events to you, my friend, that will live forever in my mind, as they ultimately led up to my becoming a patch-holding member of the Hell's Angels Motorcycle Club, so here we go.

"A brouhaha in the club got started when Lonesome's wife got slapped by some guy who supposedly had a longtime beef with her. The guy knew very well that Lonesome was the vice president of the Hell's Angels Nomads at the time. When the guy and some other enemies of the club pulled up behind his wife at a stop light, he got out and walked over to her and slapped her through her open window, that was it.

"Naturally, there had to be retribution. It was all very intentional and disrespectful as hell and amounted to an act of total fucking war!

"Lonesome's wife had gotten their plate number, so we were able to get the name and home address of the driver through our official connections, and once we confirmed that the driver and the individual who had committed the assault lived together at the house with some other friends, it was only a question of what exactly was to be done.

"We met at Lonesome's house in Sacramento to discuss the matter, and words flew hot and heavy. The outlaw-biker world was waiting to see what we were going to do. The Hell's Angels had pillaged and burned and changed the physical condition of many individuals forever by way of repayment for far less serious offenses, so who knew what the fuck was going to happen now?

Lonesome yelled out that we should just barge into

their fucking living quarters and beat the living shit out of anybody we found there, and that was the plan that was decided on. Us against them, right out in the open, with no secret who-done-it bullshit involved.

"It was the stupidest battle plan ever devised! Barging into their house would, without question, result in every one of us either being killed, seriously maimed, or sent to prison for a very long period of time. No other reasonable outcome could be expected. We knew they'd be armed and ready for us at all times, and we sure as hell would be armed to the teeth as well, so there was no question that some heavy shit was going to come down.

"Please keep in mind that I had only recently become a prospect, after a few months of being just a hang-around, so I couldn't vote and wasn't expected to say anything at meetings. I just couldn't hold back, though. I yelled out from the rear how stupid the plan was. I told them in very clear terms what I just told you, that everybody who went on the charge into that apartment would either end up behind bars for a good long time or be deader than hell for even longer.

"A vote was taken, though, and it was decided that we'd attack that night, so I jumped on board. What the fuck, it's going to happen anyway, I thought. So I raised my arm and started screaming, 'Hell's Angels forever!' and before long everyone else was screaming it along with me. I can still hear that roar, man! It was so damned exciting. It was like being with my Viking ancestors on the verge of a major battle!

"When you're part of something like that your primordial instincts kick in big time and you'll do absolutely anything for the pack, and right away I got my chance to prove myself.

"'So, Jake' Lonesome yelled out, 'since you're so

much for this little action all of a sudden, you're going to be the one to lead the charge!'

"Damn! I knew it was pure suicide. I sure as hell knew a bad plan when I saw one but, just like I've always done at critical times in my life, I went right straight for it.

"'Yes, sir!' I yelled, 'My pleasure! Just let me know when and where, sir!'

"After I said that, everybody started roaring their heads off, stomping their boots on the floor and throwing beer bottles against the walls. That's when you knew something big was coming down with the Hell's Angels. When they started stomping on the floor and throwing beer bottles against the walls, look the fuck out!

"After everything quieted down a bit, Lonesome came over to me and filled me in on the details of the plan. Oh, they were brilliant. To begin with, everyone but me was going to be armed. I wasn't going to need a gun because I was going to be used as a human battering ram, Lonesome explained.

"So, here's how it went down: Six of us, all armed but me, arrive at the house at the stroke of midnight a couple of nights later. We didn't have any idea of how many men were going to be on the other side of the door. There could have been twenty of them. Or, for all we knew, every one of them might have done the smart thing and booked it for the Fiji Islands.

"The plan was for me to knock, then when someone answered the door I was to reach in and grab him and turn him around and hold him out in front of us as a shield as we charged into the house. The thinking was that having their buddy in front of us like that would deter them from firing at us, or at least cause them to hesitate a bit. My Hell's Angels brothers had every confidence in my ability to grab onto whoever came to the door and manipulate them any way I wanted to. Oh, man, I might have oversold myself to these guys, I was thinking.

"Okay, I was at the door with five of my Hell's Angels brothers behind me, all heavily armed with handguns, and a couple of them with heavy chains as well. I knocked quite lightly, so as not to alarm anyone inside, and after a moment the door started to open very slowly and I saw that the person on the other side was a very slender teen age kid, who appeared to be about seventeen years old. He was extremely nervous and had a look of bewilderment on his face that instantaneously conveyed to me that he had no idea what was going on. I instinctively felt sorry for him, and instead of grabbing him and using him as a shield, I took hold of his shoulders and shoved him into a coatroom on the left side. That, without a doubt, saved his life, because as soon as I shoved the kid out of the way we came under fire from a guy who had popped out of a bedroom down the hall. When one of my brothers immediately yelled that he was the one who had slapped the woman, we knew we had our man.

"As soon as the guy appeared, I started running crouched over down the hall towards him, while he continued to fire at me. Bullets were also flying over my shoulder from my brothers behind me, then, out of nowhere, a woman pops out of a bedroom on the right and runs at me, screaming hysterically at the top of her voice for us to get the hell out of her house. I wasn't about to use a woman as a shield, any more than I would a seventeen-year-old kid, of course, so I quickly shoved her back into the bedroom and continued charging at the guy with the pistol. I later found out that he fired nine shots at us in the hallway, wounding three of my Hell's Angels brothers, two of them critically, and one of the bullets might have creased my scalp, I'm not sure.

"When he saw that he hadn't stopped me, the guy ran back into the bedroom, probably thinking that I wouldn't follow him, because he was armed and I wasn't. He had seen me chivalrously push the woman out of the way, so he might have come by a mistaken idea of the kind of maniac he was dealing with. Before I could get to him, though, he got two more shots off. He had the pistol leveled right at me, but no dice, I just kept coming, and when I got close enough I jumped him and slammed him against a wall and started beating the fuck out of him.

"Truthfully, though, I didn't think he deserved to die for what he had done. He had just slapped a woman, after all. It would have been sufficient for me to have sought him out somewhere and beat the piss out of him, like I have done to women beaters on many occasions, so I really wasn't hell bent on beating him to death or anything.

"I didn't have time to really do the guy up bad anyway, though," Jake continued. "We had three wounded and my other brothers were screaming that we needed to get them to a hospital, so that's all I could think of, and I just knocked the guy out, instead of beating him to death."

TO THE HOSPITAL

"My most seriously wounded brother was writhing in agony on the floor, and we were so frantic to get him to a hospital that we just left the bad guy I had beaten to a pulp lying unconscious on the bedroom floor and got the hell out of there as quickly as we could. As we were exiting, I caught sight of the woman and the kid huddled together in the bedroom. I think they were mother and son, and they were obviously very grateful just to be alive.

"When we got to the emergency room parking lot, the nurses and orderlies didn't seem to understand the seriousness of the situation right away, so I ran down a hallway where I saw three stretchers lined up, and with blood from a scalp wound streaming down my forehead and the side of my face, I commandeered the three stretchers and wheeled them out into the parking lot. When a young doctor demanded to know what I was doing, I grabbed him by the shoulders and spun him around and pushed him towards my three wounded brothers. That bit of roughness with the young doc didn't go down too well with the other medical personnel in the area, as one might suppose would be the case, and the police were called.

"In all the confusion, I wasn't even aware that I'd been shot. I still don't know when I was hit, I think it was when I was charging down the hall at the guy, but it might have been when I ran into the bedroom and tackled him. Anyway, it was only a slight scalp wound, but with all that blood running down from my forehead over my face, I was a very dramatic sight.

"At that point I could have ducked away from the hospital and no one would have ever known that I had taken part in the invasion of the house. The whole thing would have been over, as far as my involvement was concerned, but instead I hung around the emergency room tending to my brothers until the police arrived. They arrested me as soon as they laid eyes on me, which I knew they would, of course. I didn't care about what was happening to me, though. Even when they had the cuffs on me and were stuffing me into the back seat of a cop car I was yelling out to the doctors and nurses to make sure to take good care of my brothers.

SACRAMENTO COUNTY JAIL

"When we got to the jail and I was being led to a holding cell, a newspaper photographer took a picture of me in handcuffs with blood streaming down from my forehead and the side of my face and it appeared in a number of publications across the country. Yours truly was featured in accounts of the incident that appeared in *True Detective* magazine, and a few other publications, including a number of California news-papers.

"Please keep in mind, my friend, that, in spite of all the mayhem I had been involved in throughout my life up until that time, I had never spent any time at all in jail. But now, here I was, locked up in the Sacramento City Jail, facing some very serious charges, including armed home invasion in the nighttime with the intent to commit murder therein. They were out to nail me, big time

"As I think I mentioned to you the first time we spoke, my father was running for re-election at the time this all transpired, and he placed an item in the Society section of the *Maine Sunday Telegram* informing family and friends that his son Jonathan was currently vacationing in California. I arranged to receive my hometown paper while I was incarcerated, and man did that little item crack me up when I came across it! I'd been telling my cellmates how ritzy my former life had been, and how my family was having difficulty explaining my present circumstances, and here was proof of everything I'd been telling them!

"Some vacation! Like I said, in spite of all the wild and stupid-assed things I had done in my life, I had never even seen the inside of a jail. That was quite re- markable, actually, but, as we shall see, it was far from my last period of incarceration. We shall get into all that happy horseshit as we go along here, but for the moment, let me tell you a little story about my first night in jail."

FIRST NIGHT JITTERS

"I did not like the sound of that cell door closing be- hind me. I was a damn prisoner, man. I was a damn prisoner. From the very beginning, I knew that I could never adjust to life on the inside, and would never be a model prisoner, so I was afraid that I'd never get out. You also have to keep in mind that I had other and even more urgent things on my mind as well. I had a severely wounded Hell's Angels brother in the hosp- ital, and I knew that two other brothers had been hit too, and I didn't know where they were or how they made out.

To make matters worse, there was an absolute maniac in the cell down the hall who had heard that there was a Hell's Angel locked up with him, and he carried on all night long about how he was going to tear me apart in the morning when they opened the cells to take us to breakfast!

Photo taken of Jake as he was being led into Sacramento County Jail after the "suicide charge." Note the blood streaming down his forehead.

JAKE

"He was a lifer who was in for some brutal murder, and they were bringing him to court to rat on a cellmate about something the guy told him. That, of course, makes him the lowest form of life in the prisoner hierarchy, but he knew beyond a doubt that maiming or killing a Hell's Angel would get him enough prestige throughout the prison system to maybe offset his having ratted on a cellmate.

"I was scared, no question about it. When you know you're going to have to fight some demented Neanderthal in the morning, it doesn't matter how strong you are, or how vicious a fighter you are, you're scared all night long, especially if it's your first night in jail.

"I paced all night, thinking about what I knew I had to do, and I decided that I'd do what I'd always done, which is to immediately take matters into my own hands, go right for whatever it is with great gusto, and accept the consequences, whatever they may be.

"They let him out of his cell in the morning just before they let me out of mine, and I knew he was across the hall waiting to rush me, so the first thing I did when the guard opened my cell was push him aside and charge across the corridor and hit the guy with a flying tackle. The guards had been hearing him yell all night about what he was going to do to me, so they were expecting something, but they thought they'd be pulling him off me. Think again, boys. After I tackled the guy and knocked him down, I wrapped my hand around the back of his neck and picked him up and bashed his head against an old iron radiator that was in the hall. Repeatedly. He didn't have much of a pulse when they finally got around to pulling me off him. I never did find out what the extent of his injuries were. Maybe I saved the State of California the costs of a lifetime incarceration, who knows. I never got charged for anything. Didn't hear a thing about it either way. Everyone in the prison system knew he had it coming, and they must have made up some kind of story. Truly, I don't know or care either way."

A PATCH-HOLDING MEMBER
OF THE HELL'S ANGELS!

"When I was being held at the Sacramento County Jail my state of mind was greatly improved by the contents of a letter I received one day. In consideration of my heroic and selfless actions having to do with leading the suicide charge into the house where the enemies of the club resided, and in consideration of the fact that I disregarded my own best interests by staying at the hospital to ensure that my Hell's Angels brothers got proper medical treatment, I had been voted in as a patch-holding member of the Hell's Angels Motor-cycle Club while I was still in jail!

"As far as I know, I had become a member of the Hell's Angels after the shortest time spent as a pros-pect in the history of the club!

"The prison personnel were telling me that I'd better get a good lawyer, that I was facing a very long prison term, maybe life, but it didn't matter to me! I had become a patch-holding member of the Hell's Angels!

"The picture of me with blood streaming down from my forehead tells the whole story. If you take close notice, my friend, you will see that I'm smiling. Smiling! And I'm being locked up for the first time in my life!

"I call it my 'Mona Lisa Smile.' The difference between her smile and mine, though, was that no one quite knows for sure what she's smiling about, and I can tell you for damn sure what I was smiling about!

"What you have to understand is that even before I got the letter from the Hell's Angels informing me that I had been accepted into the club as a patch holding member, I knew that I had done something extra-ordinary for the club and that I would surely be recognized for it. That's what my smile was all about. Hell, I had spoken up against the suicide charge into the apartment, but when it was decided that that's what we were going to do, I led the damn charge! Then, after we charged into the apartment and exchanged fire with the enemy, I could have deserted my brothers and saved myself, and no one would have known that I had even been there. Instead, I stayed and made sure that my wounded brothers got to the hospital, and I also could have cut out when we arrived at the hospital, but instead I stuck around and made sure they received proper treatment. The Hell's Angels loved me for what I did! What's not to smile about? I had fulfilled my destiny! I had become a member of the most exclusive club on the planet! Striding into gun fire apparently gets your application for membership moved to the top of the pile!

"HELL'S ANGELS FOREVER!"

Hell's Angels leaving the San Quentin parking lot. This picture is a copy of one taken by the prison guards, who were looking for parole violators. Jake got this copy for five packs of Camel cigarettes.

Newspaper photo of Jake and some fellow Hell's Angels heading to jail after the suicide charge. Jake says his only regret is that this picture doesn't show the blood streaming down his face from the scalp wound he received.

NINE

There we were, in the backyard of the Munjoy Hill Tavern again. It was kind of understood between us that we'd be meeting there while we were talking about Jake's days with the Hell's Angels. We never had more than one or two beers at the tavern, though. It wasn't about the drinking, it was all about setting and atmosphere. This time we met there on one of those nice sunny afternoons with the scent of the ocean in the air that Portland is known for, and with the colorful local history mural on the wall, the scene for our talk was set. It also helped that the owner of the place was so eager to have us there. He was honored, in fact, and that meant a lot, especially to Jake.

"Let's hope our ol' buddy Stan shows up today," he said as we sat down at our regular table. "He reminds me of our friend the alpha-male seagull from the top of the parking garage. He'd have your ass no matter what, in a fight or whatever, every time, no questions asked. There's an integrity about him that I like. He's not like me, he's not the violent type, he's a gentle and humble man. But he'd be right there with you no matter what shit came down. You'd better believe it. Stan's a friend all the way, right to the end, and he is as strong as a bull!"

The circle grows. The people in his building, the seagull from the parking garage, me, and Stan.

"Okay, Jake," I said, after a little pause, "let's get to it. The last time we tuned in you were twenty-eight years old, had been arraigned on multiple felony charges, and were in Sacramento County Jail, which was the first time in your life you had been behind bars. So let's take it from there, please."

"I was released on bail from Sacramento County Jail after about two weeks," he dutifully responded. "The authorities told me that my trial would be in the third week of August, that they had a huge amount of evidence against me, and that, depending on how things went, I could be facing five years to life.

"Five years to life," he explained, "was a California crime-fighting initiative put forward by extreme law and order advocate Governor Ronald Reagan, whereby convicted felons served a minimum of five years, and were released only when they'd shown by their good behavior in prison that they could be a good citizen on the outside. I knew, of course, that I could never be a good citizen anywhere, inside prison or out, so I was well aware that I was looking down the barrel at doing what was called 'life on the installment plan.'"

So there he was, I was thinking, this exceedingly robust, totally in love with life twenty-eight year old guy from a prominent family who's faced with the prospect of spending the rest of his life in prison. Absolutely no freedom to come and go. No women in his life. A lifetime spent behind cell bars and prison walls, with only other men as company. I could only imagine what the prospect of that that must have felt like to someone with his appetites and sensibilities. I asked him in a hushed voice to maybe talk a little bit about what he was going through emotionally at that time.

He burst out laughing! He thought it was funny as hell that I'd be concerned about his state of mind!

"Ha! You are failing to consider something that is very basic here, my friend!" he roared. "Something that completely overruled and eliminated any feelings of dread I might have had about spending the rest of my life in prison!"

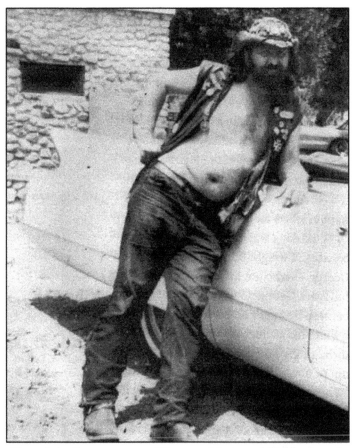

Chocolate George, one of the most beloved Hell's Angels, whose death in 1967 inspired a procession of bikers that stretched for blocks.

This photo of the Hell's Angels riding in a funeral procession for Chocolate George, a brother who had been killed in a motorcycle accident, became a very well-known poster around the world, and was especially popular in the outlaw biker world.

After leaning back and sitting there shaking his head back and forth a little, chuckling to himself like he just couldn't grasp the degree of my denseness, he looked over at me in amused exasperation and spoke slowly and deliberately, carefully enunciating each word, so that I'd be sure to get it this time: "I'd become a patch-holding member of the Hell's Angels Motorcycle Club while I was in Sacramento County Jail!"

I looked at him blankly, not quite believing what I was hearing. I hadn't forgotten what he had told me about getting the letter from the Hell's Angels while he was in jail, but I just hadn't been able to accept that his becoming a patch-holding member of the Hell's Angels was more important to him than whether or not he was going to spend the rest of his life in prison. It definitely was, though.

Jake took this picture of some Hell's Angels partying with members of The Galloping Goose Club, a long-time outlaw biker club from Los Angeles that is respected by the Hell's Angels.

Hell's Angels Nomads in 1964, just before Jake joined the club. Jake says he never did meet the three angels on the left, but that he met his brother Springtime, on the second Harley from the right, in Susanville State Prison, and that while there Springtime gave him his Hell's Angels tattoo. On Springtime's left is Jim "Mother" Miles, who Jake says was the very respected president of the Nomads. Mother Miles was killed in a motorcycle accident about two years after this photo was taken, and his funeral was attended by so many outlaw bikers from across the country that it made the national news.

JAKE

"I was over the moon when I got that letter informing me that I'd been voted into the Hell's Angels! I could hardly feel my body! I just kept pacing back and forth in my cell, trying to absorb the news and imagining what being with my Hell's Angels brothers would be like when I got out of jail on bail! I'd sit back down on my bunk and read the letter again for the umpteenth time and jump up and scream with excitement every time, just the way I did the first time I read it!

"I had been accepted into the most exclusive club in the world! I had realized my destiny! I had bonded forever with the toughest men on the planet, just like my Viking ancestors Rollo and William the Conqueror had done! Professional researchers have found them both in my family tree. When I rode with my Hell's Angels brothers, I felt like my illustrious ancestors must have felt when they led their armies rampaging and pillaging all across the face of the known earth and beyond! My whole life had been leading up to exactly what I was experiencing at that time!

"From the time I got that letter, I never gave the trouble I was in another thought. All I could think of was walking out the front door of that place and being with my Hell's Angels brothers. Then a guard shows up and tells me that one of my brothers has bailed me out! I almost picked the guy up and kissed him! When I walked out of the front door of Sacramento County Jail with one of my Hell's Angel brothers by my side I felt like I was stepping into heaven!"

Hell's Angels? Heaven? The two are connected for him? I couldn't help thinking about the struggle for his soul he said took place between the angels from Heaven and the angels from Hell when he almost froze to death in Death Valley some years earlier.

"They let me out on bail for the five months prior to my trial date in August," he continued, "and it was the most glorious five months of my life! I did not give one fucking thought to my upcoming trial all summer long! And none of my brothers said a word about it, ever!

"I had hung out with the Hell's Angels a lot, and I had even been on a number of long runs with them, but I had just been a hang-around, then a prospect, which meant that I was not really one of them. But becoming a patch-holding member was like the difference between a friendship ring and a wedding ring, you know?"

He looked at me the way guys do when they tell each other about their love lives.

"It was unheard of to become a member in less than two years, and some guys went through three or more years of hell waiting to be voted in! But I became an official prospect in late February and became a patch-holding member by the Ides of March!"

"I was a member of the Nomad chapter, which was the most violent of all the Hell's Angels chapters. Most of the members in the other chapters had a job, some even had families, but none of the Nomads were regularly employed. Our Hell's Angels brothers were the only real family we had. The Nomads hung out together all day and night, and often crashed in the same places. We got to know each other very well. There wasn't any rivalry among us about the things that mattered, we put the welfare of a brother above our own, at all times. And your brother is always right because he's your brother. Period.

"We'd kick the shit out of each other now and then, sure, but it was just because we liked to fight. We didn't mean anything by it. The only rule was that you

didn't punch a brother in the face. Hey, you don't want
a guy waking up every morning for the next forty years
with a pain shooting across his face just because his
brother got a little rambunctious fucking around one
night. See, we had some sense! Sure we did!"

He looked over at me as if I might have thought
otherwise, but I just shrugged my shoulders and kept
writing.

"When I became a member of the Hell's Angels I felt
held by something bigger than myself. I was seen for
who I was, not for who I pretended to be. I didn't
change one frigging thing about my real self to become
a Hell's Angel. They accepted me for who I was, right
from the beginning. Here was someone very different
from them, but they accepted me for just who I am
because I put myself out there to them truthfully and
honestly and in the spirit of true and everlasting
brotherhood."

"Okay, Jake," I said, "that's great, but what was it
like hanging around with the Hell's Angels on a daily
basis? I mean, what did you guys do, I mean, you
know ..."

"Oh, there was a lot of just hanging around working
on our bikes and going for rides," he answered, "but
there were practical matters to attend to, fights that
had to be fought, that sort of thing. Some of us
allegedly made our living by engaging in activities
outside the law, and that made certain demands on
our time as well. My alleged specialty was stealing cars
and motorcycles and selling them for whatever profit I
could get. It was the same one-hundred per-cent profit
business plan I had developed years before, and I'm
happy to say that it had stood the test of time. Don't
get the impression that my life was filled with nothing
but grueling hard work, though. I did manage to have

some fun from time to time."

"Okay, Jake," I said, "how about a good story that took place when you were hanging with the Hell's Angels? Something that desribes what was it like being with them from day to day, you know?"

DIRTY DELBERT

"Okay, I get it, here ya go," he began. "Once upon a time a brother named Dirty Delbert and I decided to get shots for the clap, due to the fact that we'd been screwing anything that could walk for a long time, without any concern about sexually transmitted diseases. That's just the way we lived. Women who had hitch-hiked across the country to fuck Hell's Angels were always coming into the Luau Club looking to fuck Sonny first, but they were happy as hell to settle for us if he wasn't around. We even had a storage room we emptied out and used for the pur-pose. Just threw an old mattress on the floor, you know how that goes. Somehow or other, though, in a rare moment of clarity and good sense, it occurred to Delbert and me that it might be wise to address the matter of sexually acquired diseases. Generally, we laughed at danger, no matter what form it took. Like when you've got your Harley up to 110 mph going around a curve on a mountain road, and you're leaning your bike so much that your body is about a foot from the pavement. You know you're most likely going to crash and burn, but you try for 120 mph anyway, which was an extremely cool feeling. But the thought of having VD is kind of creepy. Having your equipment rot away slowly but surely is not cool, so we decided to pay a visit to a VD clinic that was in the neighborhood of the clubhouse.

"There were about a dozen guys waiting in line for shots when we got there, but Hell's Angels don't wait in line for any reason, that just doesn't happen, so we just plodded up to the front of the line and told the pretty little nurse that we were there to get our shots.

"She smiled sweetly and said she was happy to see us, but that we'd have to go to the end of the line. She was accustomed to being listened to very respectfully by the men who went there because they were feeling very meek, considering the circumstances, so she was startled when we didn't immediately comply with her directive. I told her that we were indeed very charmed by her, and wished to cooperate, but that we were on a mission from the Lord and didn't have a moment to spare.

"That's when she got on the intercom and summoned the attending physician. Delbert and I took that to mean that he was the one who was going to be giving us our shots, so by the time the young doctor arrived we had our jackets off, ready to go into the next room with him to drop our pants and get the needle in the ass.

"When it became apparent that that wasn't happening, and he told us that we needed to go to the end of the line, I didn't say a thing. I just looked at him in a very confused way and lifted my jacket off the back of the chair and showed him the Hell's Angels insignia on the back.

"Right away he kind of gulped and cleared his throat and mumbled something about having a Harley himself and how happy he was to meet us, but that we'd have to go to the back of the line just the same.

"That's when I started acting real offended, like my

feelings were very hurt, and I told him in a very stern but friendly way that if we didn't get our shots right then, Delbert and I were going to leave the clinic immediately and go absolutely berserk giving the clap to as many women as possible, and we'd encourage all our Hell's Angels brothers to do the very same thing.

"The doctor was evidently familiar enough with the Hell's Angels to know that we were extremely promiscuous, even when we weren't on a mission to avenge an insult paid to two patch-holding brothers. And he also knew that most of the women hitch-hiking across America to fuck Hell's Angels weren't really all that discriminating about who they might have sex with after that, so there was no limit on how many men they might infect. He did the exponential math on that one, I'm sure, and could see the nightmare he was creating by being so darn stubborn about not giving us our shots.

"Give 'em their shots" he said to the nurse under his breath as he scooted back into his office, being careful to avoid eye contact with the guys behind us in line. I yelled after him that I hoped we'd see him out on the highway on his Harley someday, and he just waved his hand without looking back at me and kept walking with his head down. The guys waiting in line hadn't said anything through the whole thing, which was very wise of them, I think. Not so much as a frown, actually, so everything was good all around. People can be very pleasant and accommodating when they decide to be."

JAKE

A picture Jake took in 1966 of from left: Terry the Tramp, Barbara (Jake's Girlfriend) and Dirty Delbert. Jake says Terry grabbed Barbara's ass just as he clicked the shutter.

This photo of some Hell's Angels and a lady friend appeared in the family-oriented, nationally circulated magazine The Saturday Evening Post, November, 1965, a time when Main Street America was very concerned about the attraction young counter-culture women seemed to have for outlaw-bikers.

JAKE

ROCK STARS AS WANNABE FRIENDS

"There's no way I can adequately describe for you what being with my Hell's Angels brothers was like. You can imagine what it does for a young man's ego to be an exception to social norms and be the absolute center of adulation of the general public, while at the same time being part of an extremely close and well-knit band of brothers. It was as if I was presented with two perfect universes to live in, and was somehow getting to live in them both at the same time.

"Mind-blowing things happened continually with the Hell's Angels. It was non-stop. Most Friday nights, for instance, after we got out of 'church,' by which we meant our regular weekly meetings at our clubhouse, we'd get on our bikes and ride to the Fillmore Auditorium, where rock groups were performing. We never paid an admission charge anywhere, of course, and we were always invited to help ourselves to the band food. Oh, wait, I can't remember if that's the way it went, but the food was good. Rock stars get only the best. Sometimes the food would all be gone before they even got down off the stage, though. They were usually nice enough not to say anything about it, which was very gentlemanly of them. Sometimes we attracted more groupies than they did anyway, so it's not a good idea to mess with the magic, you know?

"We hung out pretty regularly with Gracie Slick and Jerry Garcia, and got to know most of the Grateful Dead. They performed at The Fillmore Auditorium pretty regularly and we went to a lot of their gigs. There was a small alcove on the right-hand side of the stage, behind the curtains, where we could sit and watch the show and see the audience through the curtains, but the audience couldn't see us. At least I don't think they could. We didn't care much either way. We'd either bring a few camp followers with us, or the bands would line up some ladies eager to make our acquaintance, and there we'd be, getting blow jobs while we watched the show, watching thousands of people screaming their heads off for us, or maybe it was for both the rock stars and us, I don't know. Anyway, it was very heady stuff, believe me."

"Oh, Jake, please-e-e ..." I moaned.

"Right on!" he roared. "I'll try to stifle that shit! Oh, but man, let me tell you, the whole Hell's Angels trip was the ultimate fucking fantasy and my brothers and I were living it just by being ourselves! We didn't worry about pleasing anybody and that's why everybody loved us!

"The best part of it all for me, though, was being out on a California freeway riding in formation with my brothers. I'll never forget the roar of a couple dozen very powerful customized "choppers" being revved up all at once, that hot California sun beating down on you, the smell of all that exhaust, and that deep rumble that seems to start way down in the ground and pounds up through your entire body. The experience will always will be with me! Hell's Angels forever!

"Man, that five month period from when I was released from Sacramento County Jail in the spring to the time of my trial in late August was the best period of time in my entire life!"

JAKE

THE TRIAL

As everyone knows, though, summers are not endless, after all, even for Hell's Angels, so Jake's August court date was bound to arrive. I asked him if it was time to talk about the trial.

"You bet! We're going to be talking about a very critical event in my life! Keep in mind, my friend, that I had never been to court for anything in my life before, and now here I was, going to trial on multiple felony charges that could put me away for a real long time.

"Four of us brothers were put on trial at the same time, and the verdicts were a foregone conclusion. It was the wild and wooly sixties, the establishment was gasping for survival, and the Hell's Angels represented everything middle America was terrified of. If the Hell's Angels could charge into someone's house with clubs, chains, and guns in the middle of the night with the intention of committing felonious assault on the occupants, and pretty much get away with it, society was doomed. So we were convicted without much delay and thrown into the holding tank of the Sacramento County jail to await sentencing.

"The trial did provide a chuckle or two, though. Hey, I'll take any stage, you know what I mean?"

I had brought along an excerpt from an account of the trial in the book *Hell's Angels*, by Jan Hudson, and I read it aloud to Jake:

Jonathan Sawyer's testimony introduced a bit of levity to the proceedings when he announced that he was a member of the Junior Chamber of Commerce, as well as of the Hell's Angels. The two organizations are probably not mutually exclusive, but the imagination boggles at the thought of a mangy looking Hell's Angel and a gray-flannel-suited young executive of the Junior Chamber of Commerce type combined in one individual.

Sawyer said he had become a Junior Chamber of Commerce member in his home state of Maine some years ago, and had only recently become a member of the Hell's Angels. In fact, he said proudly, he had received a letter while he was in Sacramento County Jail telling him that his membership in the Hell's Angels had been approved.

Under questioning by District Attorney Riley, Sawyer acknowledged that he was a weight lifter, and that he weighed 210 pounds and stood six-feet, two-inches tall, but denied that he was known to the Hell's Angels as "Bonecrusher."

"The District Attorney was the first one to call me 'Bonecrusher!' Jake boomed when I finished reading. "He made the name up himself! Every Hell's Angel has a moniker and my Hell's Angels brothers either called me 'Jake from Maine' or 'Jake the Dancer.' There wasn't any damn 'Bonecrusher' involved at any time until that damn District Attorney hung the name on me!

"Anyway, Bonecrusher was the name I became known by after the District Attorney stuck it on me at the trial. I can't tell you how many fights I've gotten into since just because of that friggin' name! It almost got me killed more than a few times in prison. I had both white guys and black guys trying to kill me. I always got along great with the Mexicans, though, because they were more interested in killing each other!"

JAKE

BACK TO SACRAMENTO COUNTY JAIL

"So there we were after the trial, three of my Hell's Angels brothers and me, thrown into a holding cell of the Sacramento County Jail to await sentencing, each having been convicted of two counts of felonious assault, and one count of first degree breaking and entering in the nighttime with intent to commit felonious assault therein.

"The whole thing seemed kind of unreal to us, actually. Something to be understood here is that the members who were chosen by the club to take part in the suicide charge were all members who had clean, or nearly clean, police records. We pretty much knew that the brothers who raided the home of our enemies were going to be facing some serious charges subsequently, and we figured that the system wasn't going to come down very hard on first time offenders, so we weren't really all that worried about what our sentences might be. Maybe a year and a half in a minimum security country club correctional facility, something like that, we figured.

"I was the first one they came and took away for sentencing, and I was shocked when I heard what I got. Six to ten years each on the two felonious assault charges, and five years to life on the breaking and entering in the nighttime with the attempt to commit felonious assault therein charges! Five years before I'd even be eligible for parole! I didn't feel a thing until I was halfway back to my cell, then it came to me that I was probably going to be spending the rest of my life in prison. With Governor Reagan's 'five years to life' crime-fighting initiative very much in effect, I was thinking that I might never be released.

"I started laughing. I actually started laughing, like the fucking idiot that I am. I don't know why I started laughing, I just did. The whole thing seemed so preposterous. What the hell had everything I'd been through in my life meant if I was going to end up spending the rest of my life in a cell? The whole thing just didn't make sense.

"When the guys waiting their turn to go get sentenced saw me laughing when I returned, they assumed that I got a very light sentence, of course, and one of them them yelled out, 'C'mon, Bone-crusher, how did it go?'

"Right away I was pissed, because a brother had called me by the stupid name the damn District Attorney stuck on me, so I yelled back: 'Piece of cake! See you at the Luau Club tonight!'

"So when the other guys got the same sentence as I did, you can imagine their shock. They didn't see the humor in my misleading them, either. They were mad as hell at me when they got back from seeing the judge which, of course, I loved, because we'd do anything to pull a real good joke on each other, and I really got them that time. I got a big kick out of welcoming them back one by one and innocently asking them what sentence they had gotten. Actually, I've been chuckling about it for years. I really am an asshole sometimes, huh?"

I chose not to respond to that one, and just kept pen to paper.

JAKE

Jake's Hell's Angel brother 'Lonesome' with an un-identified 'friend.' Jake says Lonesome was a genius mechanic and motorcycle designer, who was especially known for the fantastic Harley choppers he built, like the one he's straddling in this picture.

TEN

After having met at the Munjoy Hill Tavern for our last three sessions, we decided we'd go back to meeting at Jake's apartment because we were both comfortable there and because the memorabilia all over his walls set the perfect tone for our talks. We knew we'd most likely return to the Munjoy Hill Tavern at some point, though. Somehow or other, we both liked that Stan understood the significance of what we were up to, and we had grown very fond of the backyard of his tavern.

"Awright, Jake," I said, after we got settled into our chairs facing each other across his living room, like before. "So now you were looking at a minimum of twenty-five years in prison, which you were probably going to stretch into life even if you made it through the twenty-five years. You went from a fantastic summer of hanging with the Hell's Angels to sitting in a cell at San Quentin Prison, huh?"

VACAVILLE

"No, my friend," he answered, a little impatiently, "the penal system doesn't operate quite that efficiently. I had to work my way up to San Quentin. We were kept at the county jail for the first three weeks after the trial, then they told us we were going to be transferred to a prison in a small town named Vacaville, located about thirty-five miles outside of San Francisco, where we would be evaluated for placement within the California prison system.

JAKE

"I have always taken a great interest in the local history of every place I've spent time, including the places where I was incarcerated over the years, and it might interest you to know that "vaca" is Italian for "cow" and that Vacaville was founded by Italian immigrant dairymen who provided the growing city of San Francisco with plenty of fresh steaks and variety of fresh dairy products. So there."

"Thanks, Jake," I said, "that'll make an interesting tidbit for the book, I guess, but let's get on with what took place with you locked up there, okay?"

"Sure! Sure!" he yelled, "but before we get to what took place at Vacaville, I should mention something that occurred before my brothers and I left Sacramento County Jail, because it might give you some insight into how well Hell's Angels tend to behave, regardless of the circumstances. It involved us tearing up our cells just because we had nothing better to do, you see. We weren't angry at the authorities or anything like that. We knew we deserved to be locked up. They had treated us fairly decently, we didn't have any particular beef with them, it was just that we were bored and needed something to do. We made an absolute shambles of all the beds and bedding and the shelves, but the most fun was uprooting and destroying all the sinks and toilets. There was about six inches of water in our cells and out in the corridor before they got the water main turned off. We really didn't mean to cause anyone any grief, we were just bored out of our minds on a quiet Saturday afternoon and tearing up our cells was just kind of a way to liven things up. It did too! Those guards were as mad as hornets at a dog that's digging up their nest!

"Transferring four Hell's Angels from Sacramento County Jail to Vacaville was quite an exciting affair too. I loved every minute of it. Ah, the splendor and the glory of it all!

"They were afraid that our Hell's Angels brothers were going to attack whatever conveyance they used to transfer us, in an attempt to free us. They also knew that the Hell's Angels had become counter-culture heroes, which meant that every aspect of our captor's treatment of us would be closely scrutinized by the liberal media. No warden or any other prison official wanted Dan Rather from CBS News sticking a microphone in his face.

"We went in a line of eight unmarked police cars, four of which contained a single shackled prisoner sitting in the back seat between two heavily armed police officers. Each car containing a prisoner had cars in front and in back of them, each with four heavily armed guards in them. All the time we were driving the officers in each car were scanning the rooftops for snipers and were in constant radio contact with helicopters in the air. Whenever they'd hear the roar of a motorcycle, or maybe a loud pop from one of their own cars running over a bottle or something, their eyes would dart all around out the window and they'd clutch their rifles a little closer. It was fun to watch them."

He was having fun, he was actually having fun, I was thinking.

"When we got to the Prison at Vacaville," he continued, "they marched us right to the warden's office, which, we found out later, was not at all the usual procedure. Most prisoners don't ever see the warden in his office, but we sure as hell did. We stood around his desk in shackles, with guards next to and behind each of us, and he gave us a very tough, straight from the shoulder talking to, the gist of which was that we were no longer in county jail, we were in the state prison system, so things would be very different now on. The administration at Sacramento County Jail had gone to the trouble of taking pictures of the damage we had done to their facility, and the warden had the pictures blown up to use as communication aids in his little talk with us, so he was able to make his point very convincingly.

"What really got to me was that, right from the start, the warden looked at me in the same way my Hell's Angels brothers did the first time I walked into the Luau Club and made their acquaintance. Like, who is this guy and what the hell is he doing here?

"He had read my paperwork, of course, and he was totally baffled. To begin with, I was most likely the only one in the entire prison who didn't have any priors. Very rarely does anyone go to prison who hasn't spent time in lesser lock-ups. With all that I had done in my life, starting with stabbing that guy in the ass when I was fourteen, stealing automobiles and motorcycles on a regular basis over the years, and being a Kentucky rum runner, it is quite remarkable that I had reached age twenty-nine and had never seen the inside of a jail.

"I was also an honorably discharged veteran, didn't smoke, didn't have a problem with alcohol, didn't have any drug addictions, and was in superb physical condition. Those things alone put me in a one percent bracket in the prison population, even apart from the having no priors. All considered, I was undoubtedly unique in the entire national prison system. That's gotta count for something, right?"

"I guess so," I said.

"When the warden had finished his little talk," Jake continued, "and we were being led out the door, he called out 'Sawyer!' and when I looked over at him he started to say something, but then he stopped himself, like he was at a loss for words, and signaled for me to just keep moving. I've always wondered what he was going to say to me. He was, of course, trying to figure out what the hell I was even doing there, that I know, and even to this day I don't know what I would've given him for an answer if he had asked me."

Nor do I, I was thinking.

SUSANVILLE

"Because of my clean record, and because I hadn't committed a major crime, like a gruesome murder or something of that nature, and because I was an honorably discharged U.S. Army Paratrooper, I would have been a shoe-in for being sent to a minimum security country club facility after my sojourn at Vacaville, but because I was a Hell's Angel and had shown absolutely no sign of bending my spirit to their will during my period of incarceration, I was instead sent to a high-security prison in the middle of a desert in Northern California by the name of Susanville. I had pleasant memories of a number of Susans and Sues, but I have to say that the name of the place was all that was pleasant about Susanville.

"I had never imagined that there could be a place on earth so isolated and forlorn. Even if you managed to escape, you were visible walking across the hot sands for about three hours, if you lasted that long. The black guys used to laugh and say it wasn't fair because they'd be visible for a much longer period of time than white guys would be!

"Racial tensions were high at Susanville at the time, actually. Many of the blacks were Black Muslim followers of Malcolm X, and had become very militant in their approach to solving the country's racial problems. If I was black, I would have become a Black Muslim because they were feared in the same way the Hell's Angels were, so right away I could relate to them. The prison population at Susanville was evenly split between black and white, and the two groups kept absolutely away from each other, but I upset that little apple cart on my first day there.

"The first time I walked out onto the prison yard I was very pleased to see groups of guys lifting weights here and there because I hadn't lifted for the six months I had been incarcerated – easily the longest period of time I had gone before or have gone since.

"The groups lifting were either all black or all white, but I didn't give a shit about that. When I ascertained that the most serious lifters was a group of black guys, I went right over to join them. I was very excited because I knew right away, by the way they were lifting and by their overall demeanor, that they were a group of guys who knew how to work out at my level. That they were black men didn't even enter into it, as far as I was concerned.

"As soon as I get over to them, this huge guy with a gold front tooth gives me a wide smile and tells me that my place is over there, and he points to some white guys playing around with some weights on the other side of the yard.

"Now, I know he can see by looking at me that I'm a serious weightlifter, because he is one too, and he knows that I'm not going to get anything out of joining those guys, so I get a little agitated and go over and snatch-lift a bar with about 225 pounds of weight on it over my head, no problem.

"I told you this ain't your place, buddy!" he yelled, just as I had the weights fully extended over my head, which pissed me off, big time. Anyone who's lifted weights at all knows that you don't distract a man when he's got a loaded bar suspended over his head. Every man looking on knew that he was disrespecting me big time, no question.

"So, what could I do? I roared like a furious fucking lion, heaved the barbell about twenty feet out in front of me, then swiveled around and threw a punch at his face!

"The punching them in the face move doesn't work well when your opponent catches your fist in mid-air and squeezes your hand like it was a rubber toy, though.

"You're in, you crazy motha'fucka!" he yelled when he let go of my hand, and that was that, I was in with the black guys. He knew, just like every man on the yard knew, what it took for anybody, especially a white guy new on the scene, to take a punch at him, considering his size and the fact that we were surrounded by a bunch of other very strong black men.

"Turned out that the guy I took the punch at, Fred was his name, didn't call the shots in just the weight-lifting group, he was the leader of all the blacks in the entire prison. Fred and I got along very well. It wasn't long before I had established myself as a leader among the white guys, partly because they knew what it took for me to get along with the blacks. It kind of amused and intrigued Fred and me that between us we could get just about every prisoner in the place to do just about anything we wanted them to do.

"One day after lunch when we were working out, Fred and I got to talking about how the food in the placed sucked so bad, and one of us suggested that maybe we should call a food strike. No one would go to breakfast, we decided. Some went to breakfast anyway, though, and they got the food kicked out of their stomachs when they returned, so nobody went to breakfast the next morning.

"The warden didn't jump to and right away change the menu or anything, he wouldn't do that, of course, but it wasn't long before we were eating a whole lot better than we had been. Nothing was said about it, it just happened.

"Fred and I were so pleased with the way the breakfast strike went down that not long afterward we called a prison-wide work strike for better living conditions all around. We put out the word through the inmate population that the strike would last until our demands were met. Hey, that's what lawbreakers do, we get carried away with ourselves, what can I say?

"We got about half of our fellow prisoners to comply with the work strike for one day, which was remarkable. I'd like to say that the changes came fast and furious, and that prisoners' living conditions and rights changed dramatically as a result of our activities at Susanville, but that would be a total frigging lie. The administration's response to the work strike was to ship most of the ringleaders of the strike to other prisons, that very day. They didn't screw around. I never even heard if conditions changed in any way, actually, but at least we tried and that meant something. Anyway, Fred wasn't shipped out to another prison, just because of who he was, but I was gone from Susanville the day after the work strike, after about a six month stay.

Con 'Agitators' Sent to Quentin

Susanville

Some 32 stubborn "agitators" at the California Conservation Center here who refused to go back to work after a mattress-throwing food strike were punished yesterday by being transferred to San Quentin.

"Food was their main complaint, but the staff thinks a group of agitators promoted the strike,'' said a spokesman for the Department of Corrections in Sacramento.

The spokesman said one busload of prisoners was escorted by Highway Patrolmen to San Quentin. He said there was a "possibility" that more inmates would be transferred there.

Acting Superintendent Fred Cardona said the food strike apparently stemmed from a bad meal last Friday.

The strike began Monday in earnest when convicts refused to go to breakfast or report for work. They boycotted lunch and dinner at the mess hall and breakfast again yesterday.

Inmates threw mattresses, furniture and garbage cans from the second-story catwalks of their dormitories. An estimated $800 damage was done, but no injuries or other violence was reported.

The strike collapsed Tuesday about midday when prisoners began drifting back to work.

The Sierra conservation center trains prisoners in forestry work and those awaiting transfer to other work camps. *Our Correspondent*

Clipping from the Sacramento Bee newspaper. As one of the ringleaders of the incident, Jake and other convicts were transferred to Folsom Prison in late 1966, and from there Jake was transferred to San Quentin.

JAKE

FOLSOM PRISON

"Next stop, Folsom Prison, which they told me was just another holding facility for me on my way to my true home in the prison system, wherever that might be. Folsom was your all-time American granite block prison, built by Chinese coolie laborers in the 1870s. I can't say I was happy to be locked up in Folsom Prison, that would be pure horseshit, but I have to say that I was privileged to experience something of America's past there. I'd always felt connected to outlaws of the Old West, like Jesse James and Cole Younger, and I felt their spirits very strongly all through the place. As we go on with our little story, you'll find out that Folsom Prison wasn't the only place where I have felt connected to those heroes of the Old West, but I don't want to get ahead of myself.

"I watch the History Channel a lot these days and once I saw the cell I was in at Folsom! They ran the camera slowly over the walls and I was riveted to the TV screen! I remembered every little black wavy line that runs through those granite walls. The one-and-three-quarter-inch thick black iron door with the six-inch barred window at the top also brought back some memories. Even the bunkbed in my cell was historical. It was made out of steel in the 1870s and was still in use! It was old enough for my friends Jesse and Cole to have slept in it. It was a single cot, of course, but it had a sturdy, black iron frame. Nothing was poorly made in those days, not even prison beds. Everything about Folsom Prison felt historical. There was no running water. Twice a day a guard would come by with fresh water, and that was it.

"There were three elderly lifers at Folsom at the

time I was there who claimed that they pulled off the last stagecoach robbery in history. They said they got away with the strongbox, but there wasn't as much in it as they thought there would be, not a hell of a lot of cash, evidently. The problem was that the guy sitting next to the driver had a shotgun behind the seat and when he reached for it, blam, he was gone. The guys said they regretted having to waste him, but what could they do?

"It was great hearing their story first-hand. Kind of made me feel connected to the great desperadoes of the American West. My time at Folsom was almost like a meditative retreat for me, actually. The historic feeling of the place took me over and allowed me to gather myself for what was coming next."

SAN QUENTIN

"When they told me that my next stop would be San Quentin, I knew things were about to tighten up for me big time. But even though I knew San Quentin was run by very severe rules and regulations and housed some of the most violent offenders in the prison system, I didn't dread going there at all, for some reason."

"That's because you were one of the most violent offenders in the prison system yourself!" I cried, interrupting him and laughing. I just couldn't restrain myself.

"You're right!" he yelled, laughing too, rocking back and forth with delight.

"They had the worst offenders in the country winnowed down to just me and the other assholes I was doing time with and I was happy as hell to have made the cut!

"Well, maybe they weren't after me, I don't know, but the warden did throw me in solitary shortly after I arrived, so there you go. Didn't seem fair, but here's the story and you can decide for yourself, okay?"

I told him I'd try to be objective.

Hell's Angels exiting the San Quentin parking lot after visiting Jake and another brother incarcerated there. Jake says the picture was taken by a guard looking for parole violations in the group, and that he traded the guard five packs of Camel cigarettes for it. Front right is Sonny Barger. Front left is Jimmy, and two behind him, with the beard and long hair, is Terry the Tramp.

Two photos of Big Frank Waite, a Hell's Angel Nomad Jake met in San Quentin. "I can't tell you what having another Nomad with you in such a place meant to us both," says Jake. "Violent wannabees very often hate Hell's Angels and are known for unprovoked, cowardly attacks on them. Big Frank and I took care of business a few times together, and became very close. I cut off an enemy's nose when I worked in the morgue and gave it to him as a birthday present!"

JAKE

A WELCOME VISIT

"Okay, here you go," he beamed: "Sonny Barger, the president of the Hell's Angels at the time, and the greatest leader of men the planet has ever known, was very grateful for my part in the suicide charge, and he took special note of the fact that I didn't desert my brothers at the hospital, even when I knew the police were on their way, so he arranged a little surprise for me when he learned that I was incarcerated in San Quentin. A recounting of how I managed to make the most of that little surprise might give you some insight into how I approached life behind bars in general.

"Sonny, of course, had a very good idea of what I was going through in San Quentin. He knew that I had never been in any kind of jail before in my life, and now here I was locked up in one of the most notorious prison in the country. He also knew that the warden had ordered that I couldn't have visits from my Hell's Angels brothers. Maybe he thought they'd try to spring me, I don't know. Anyway, one visiting day shortly after I arrived, they announced over the intercom which inmates had visitors, and I was very surprised to hear my name. I couldn't believe it because I hardly knew anyone in California besides my Hell's Angels brothers, and I hadn't gone out of my way to inform the folks back home of my whereabouts, so I was very curious about what was up. When I got to the visiting room I didn't recognize anyone there, but when I looked around the room and spotted an absolutely beautiful blonde woman wearing a black mini-skirt, she was all I was interested in anyway. We're talking a twenty-nine-year-old extraordinarily healthy American male with a notoriously huge sexual appetite who, after Sacramento County Jail, Vacaville, Susanville, Folsom Prison, and now San Quentin, hadn't *seen* a woman in a very long time! Now a luscious blonde goddess had appeared in the flesh before my very eyes!

"When she saw me staring at her, she smiled demurely and lowered her gaze, appearing to be blushing, then she picked her head up and looked straight over at me with the most wanton, I-want-you-right-now look I've ever seen on a woman in my entire life! When she slowly uncrossed her legs and stood up and started walking across the room to my visitors station like she was on the boardwalk of the Miss America Beauty Pageant, all of a sudden San Quentin turned into Palisades Park!

"So then there she was, sitting a few feet across from me, with a wooden divider about a foot tall separating us. At that point I didn't care about not being able to make physical contact with her, though. Just looking at her was enough for me!

"We tried to talk a little, but she seemed to be having trouble speaking. I thought that it was just that she was nervous, but I soon found out that that wasn't the case at all. The rule was that a prisoner and his visitor were allowed one short kiss, and the procedure was for the two of you to stand up and lean over the wooden divider to accomplish that. Romantic, huh? Well, anyway, I thought that what the voluptuous yellow-haired lady across from me was trying to say was that we should kiss because her visit was a little gift from Sonny, and he'd be disappointed if we didn't at least kiss. I was all for it, of course, but as soon as we leaned in and our lips met I realized that there was yet another gift involved here! She immediately stuck her tongue in my mouth deeper than any woman ever has before or since and deposited two LSD tablets down my throat! Thank you, Sonny!

"Now that she could talk better, we had a very enjoyable conversation, mostly about Sonny's appreciation of my not having ratted on my Hell's Angels brothers. The LSD started to do its thing, though, and I was losing my ability to continue our conversation. Sonny was buddies with a well-known genius chemist who created the most potent form of LSD available, and I had ingested two tablets of what I knew to be his signature recipe.

"Now, anyone who's familiar with the tripping experience will tell you that in addition to its hallucinatory effects, LSD tends to make a person extremely horny, as if I needed to be more so at the moment! So in the midst of all this horniness there's this blonde goddess sitting across from me panting for my body as much as I am for hers. Damn, after a while we just stopped talking and just sat looking across at each other, just about drooling. Then I did it! I hopped up onto the visitors table, stepped over the fucking wooden divider, and jumped down onto the floor and muckled onto her! I can still feel her body today! We were clawing at each other like wild animals! And keep in mind that everybody in the room was watching us! My hands immediately flew up her dress, and before the guards got to us and started beating me with their Billy clubs I achieved full digital penetration! Full digital penetration, sir! When they were dragging me away one of the guards laughed and said that I'd be spending a few months in solitary on bread and water for my brief moment of pure joy, and when he asked me if it was worth it, I yelled, 'Hell, yes! Just don't make me wash my finger!' The other prisoners and their visitors applauded and cheered like mad, and even the guards cracked up.

"So that's the end of today's little love story. Bet you didn't know I had such a romantic streak in me, huh?"

"Yes, I'm very moved," I said.

LIFE IN SAN QUENTIN

"I've told you about the first night I had ever spent in jail in my life, just a few months before I went to San Quentin, with the lifer screaming all night about how he was going to kill me in the morning because I was a Hell's Angel, and how I had to bash his head into a radiator repeatedly in the morning, but this time I wasn't in county jail, I was in San Quentin, and I had five thousand people like him waiting for me to show my face! I'll never forgive that damn DA for sticking the name Bonecrusher on me – every tough guy in the place wanted a piece of me as soon as they heard that name. They all knew that whoever killed 'The Bonecrusher' would have something to brag about for the rest of their time in prison.

"Another thing that made that time in solitary especially bad for me was the thought of how my mother was feeling about me being locked in a penitentiary with a bunch of hardened criminals way across the country in California. All I could do was try to ease her mind as best I could with jokey kinds of letters, but she knew how much I loved my freedom and knew very well what I was going through.

"Most guys are in prison for a long time before they realize that you have to take your mind off the outside if you want to make a life for yourself inside. I knew it immediately, and I also knew that I had to live inside the prison like I'd always lived my life, which is to go right straight for whatever the hell it was I wanted. What I really wanted at San Quentin was to be respected, and earning respect in a hard-assed prison like San Quentin was a full-time job.

"I'd gotten my first Look at San Quentin when I was just a hang-around and went on the Petaluma "run" with the Hell's Angels. We were crossing the San Rafael Bridge over San Francisco Bay, and you could see the prison across the water. San Quentin's not like Folsom, it doesn't have any character, it looks very bleak and institutional. No charm at all. When I first saw the place, I immediately thought of all the free spirits, fellow lovers of the sun and the wind, who were locked up for the rest of their lives in such a soulless dungeon. I remember feeling guilty about all the freedom I had. Now here I was, less than a year later, locked up in the damn place!

"Truthfully, though, underneath it all, I was excited about all the experiences I was going to have. The prison psychologist told me the same thing that other mental health professionals have been telling me my whole life: that I don't feel fear the way other people do. I look at dire situations as opportunities for fun and adventure. That's not idle fucking bragging, either. It's the raw damn truth. Hey, keep in mind that I stabbed that friggin' guy at fourteen years old and enjoyed doing it!

"If I told you I sat on my bunk looking down at the floor for the first month I was there, which a lot of guys do, I'd be lying. Yeah, I sat on my bunk thinking sometimes, but it was about how to take over the place. I knew that virtually every guy in San Quentin was in there for violence-related crimes, so I'd never been more in my element.

Jake (front, center) with the weightlifting group he organized at San Quentin. He says only the top 5% of the prison population got to be Regulators and have the honor of putting their lives on the line.

JAKE

"My arrival at San Quentin was very big news among the prisoners on the yard because the Hell's Angels suicide charge had been all over the media and my picture had been in *True Detective* magazine, and what I'd done in the few months I'd been incarcerated by the State of California was also very hot news in prison yards across the country, so a lot of prisoners at San Quentin were looking forward to making my acquaintance.

"There is a breed of men, of which I am one, though, whose reflexive reaction to having an aggressive individual in their midst is to react with superior aggression, and those were the ones I was concerned about.

"As in the past, though, weightlifting and working out came to my rescue again.

"The day I got out of solitary and walked out onto the yard every eye was on me. I saw a lot of different reactions, some of which I was concerned about, some of which I wasn't, but, either way, I figured I might as well put on a show now that I had their attention.

"There was a barbell across the yard with what must have been three hundred and fifty pounds on it. The most I'd ever been able to lift was three-hundred and ten, but I said what the fuck.

"They all knew it would not be possible for someone my size to lift that much weight, and they all smirked when I positioned myself in front of the bar. When I yanked it up to my waist, they started yelling Bronx cheers and shit, like I sure as hell wasn't going to get it up to my shoulders. But, bang! I did it! After that, they were all quiet, like something amazing might happen here.

"I just didn't have enough strength to jerk it up over my head, though. I put absolutely everything I had in it, of course, but I just didn't have the body weight to do it. They could see me straining my guts out, though, putting every ounce of strength I had into it, and they were very impressed by the time I threw the damn thing down on the ground and it made a huge clanging sound and bounced like it was made of rubber.

"I got a faint round of applause for my little show – a few brave souls among them dared to show their true feelings – and that was very satisfying to me.

"After I had established myself as the psychopathic madman and self-obsessed show-off they'd been hearing so much about, they knew fucking well I'd confront any one of them head fucking straight on in anything they wanted to pull, and that was the message a boy needed to deliver if he was going to prosper in his new neighborhood.

"Life inside San Quentin was extremely tough, though, no matter how strong you were or how big your balls were. Rivalries develop in prison, of course, and the name of the game is to be able to carry through on your threats. Someone bumps into your elbow in chow line and doesn't apologize, and you don't shank him with some kind of improvised weapon, you're a marked man. A shank is any long thin sharp pointed piece of material that suffices for a knife, that can be easily concealed on one's person, by the way. If someone shoves one into you and you don't retaliate it means that anyone can do anything to you, just for fun, and your life becomes a living hell."

JAKE

THE REGULATORS

"In order to survive in prison, you need to belong to a group of men who will stick together, no matter what. Everyone in the place needs to know that if you get killed, whoever did it is going to die for it, that way no one gets killed. Most lone wolves don't last long out on the yard. Some prisoners preferred to live in isolation than be out on the yard, and the prison was obliged to accommodate them, but that's no way to live your life.

"My chosen group was obviously going to be the most serious and violent weightlifters, and shortly after my arrival I was elected chief of the group I lifted with because of the professional body-building advice I'd been able to pass on to them, but also because I could lift more, pound for pound, than any man in the place.

"I put together a little band of men I called the Regulators, which included two former paratroopers and two former Marines, who had all been convicted of some type of felonious assault charges, including murder. The mission of the Regulators was to mediate matters between the various groups in the prison, usually by deciding disputes in a way that would benefit us personally, and kicking the fuck out of anyone who didn't go along with the plan.

"Here's how it went: If you needed to retaliate for some offense against you by shanking someone, there was a procedure that needed to be followed to the greatest detail. One of our guys would come up behind the mark and grab him by the arms from the back, so that his chest stuck out, then the guy in front would do the appropriate type of shanking, whether it be a painful warning, or the down for the count kind.

"After the shanking, our guy would go straight to the outdoor john, where he washed off any blood there was on himself and on the knife, then he'd be given clean clothes by another one of our guys who passed by the john for the purpose.

"Oh, wait a minute!" Jake erupted mid-story. "Here's a remnant of my stay at San Quentin right here!"

Leaning forward in his chair, he pointed excitedly at a large and colorful tattoo on his right calf of a naked blonde woman holding onto the Devil's ears and riding his tongue. She definitely looks like she's having a good time, even after all these years, especially when Jake flexes his muscle.

"Everything we did in prison we had to do on the sly, of course, and a big part of how much respect you got was your ability to facilitate matters.

"My man Adrian was an absolute creative genius who could tattoo like a bastard if you could make it possible for him to do his thing. I got him to do the tattoo you're looking at on his knees beside me in church services one Sunday morning. We had attended services for that purpose, actually. He did his thing with a guitar string that somehow came into his possession, and I don't know where he got his dyes and India ink, but this tattoo he put on me has withstood the test of time."

There is a story to everything, I was thinking.

JAKE

THINGS START TO GO SOUTH

"So, I tried to make the best of a very bad situation at San Quentin. As has always seemed to happen in my life, though, I started to get the feeling that I had overstayed my welcome. After about six months, things started getting very toxic for me. I had alienated a number of my fellow prisoners in one way or another and the prospects for brutal retaliations were looming large.

"My relations with the prison authorities weren't looking all that good, either. Unsolved incidents of destruction of prison property and acts of violence committed within the prison population had increased noticeably since my arrival, and they knew who was responsible for a good deal of it. They couldn't pin a thing on me, but they damn well knew who was behind it all.

"We always had our ears open for any information we could use, and the more friends you had the more information you had. One of my guys washing the floor inside a stall in the head heard the warden and a guard talking while they were taking a piss, and the warden said that he knew that Sawyer was behind a lot of the unrest that was going on and they were doing their best to build a case against me.

"The guy told me that as the warden and the guy he was talking to were zipping up their flies and turning away from the urinals, the warden said: 'Yeah! We call Sawyer the *The Ghost*! When we come upon the scene of some incident we know he's been there, but we've never been able to pin it on him! Fuck it! I think it's time we pick him on general principles and put him in solitary again for a while, just to see if things get any better around here!'

"After that little conversation became known a-round the prison, the prisoners started calling me 'The Ghost,' and I didn't like that at all. Your whole cover is blown once you get a name like that pinned on you, man. The authorities start to watch you very, very closely once you get a reputation for outwitting them. It was the same thing with the Bonecrusher name that got stuck on me too, of course. You get put in a little box you can't get out of. That's why I told my guys to low-key it on calling ourselves The Regulators. The more you got puffed up about living up to some friggin' name, the more unlikely you were to regulate a fucking thing. That's just one of those little life lessons you learn. Or maybe you don't learn, who knows?

"As it turned out, the prisoners got to me before the prison authorities did. One day a guy came up behind me in the industrial alley on the lower yard and drove a shank into my back before I even knew he was there. I had had to go through that dangerous area of the prison to go to the shoe repair shop, where I went to get my orthopedic shoe repaired. It felt like a punch, I didn't feel any penetration, but I instinctively knew exactly what had occurred.

"There were shankings that are meant to be warn-ings, and there were shankings that were meant to kill. This one was not a warning, it was a botched kill. I like to think my presence alone intimidated the back-stabbing bastard but, who knows, he might just have been a clumsy fuck. He cut me pretty good, though."

At this point, Jake stood up and pulled up his shirt and showed me the two-inch long, jagged scar from the shanking, and a very queasy feeling came over me.

JAKE

LEMME OUTTA HERE

"Every effort was made to keep shankings away from the ears of the warden, of course, because when you got shanked everybody knew it was because you shanked somebody else, even if it couldn't be proven. I just didn't want to give the warden the precipitating cause he was looking for to put me in solitary confinement again, so I had to get medical treatment from sources within the prison population. The attending physician from within the prison population turned out to be Dr. Bernard Finch, who had been known as the doctor of the stars on the outside and had been convicted of having his wife killed. Dr. Finch patched me up, no problem, charged me two packs of cigarettes, and all was okay again.

"My first parole hearing was coming up in about three months and the general consensus was that they'd laugh me out of the room," Jake continued. "The oldtimers on the yard assured me that I could look forward to making the acquaintance of every person who served on the San Quentin parole board for the next half century or so, or for however long I lived.

"I was desperate, I really was, more than I had ever been in my life, and I knew that it was time for me to focus very hard on finding a way to help myself. I got to scanning my life for people I thought might help me and I came up with a lot of possibilities, but I dismissed them one after another for various reasons. Then a light went on. There was this guy from the South Portland neighborhood I grew up in who I'd always liked and respected and who I knew was currently working in Washington, D.C. at the White

House. I didn't know what he did there, but I knew he was somebody important. He's a few years older than me, so we never became buddies when we were kids, but we had encountered one another a few times since and were very friendly to one another. We enjoyed talking about the old neighborhood and mutual acquaintances, things like that.

"So I decided to write him a letter addressed to the White House explaining my situation to him. I didn't whine or beg or try to make him feel bad. I also didn't say sappy things about the old neighborhood and how fond we were of various common acquaintances. Forget that stuff. I just laid the whole thing out for him. I didn't tell him I was innocent of the charges, of course, because I sure as hell wasn't, but I made it clear to him that the harsh sentence I had received was given to me because I was a Hell's Angel and they wanted to make an example of me, in spite of the fact that I was an honorably discharged United States Army paratrooper with no prior criminal record. I also told him about how hard it was for someone with my social background, which was the same as his, to survive at a place like San Quentin, and that I felt that my life was in imminent danger.

"I made it *very* clear to him that I absolutely *would not* rat on anyone to win my release. I told him that if I never heard from him I would absolutely understand and still have the greatest regard for him. I would have, too. I understood that I had fucked up and was continuing to do so, so I deserved what I got. Hell, I had fun along the way, shouldn't there be a price to pay?"

JAKE

Picture taken by a guard looking for parole violations of a Hell's Angel and his girlfriend walking toward the east block of San Quentin. Jake says he was incarcerated in the east block for a while and could see the lights of Oakland, where the clubhouse of the Nomad chapter was located, glistening brightly down the bay at night.

A SAVIOR FROM ON HIGH

"I really didn't give much thought to the parole board hearing because I was too busy staying alive and jockeying for position in the prisoner hierarchy. Even after you've lost your taste for it all, you had to keep at it or you'd be wasted before you knew it. This was the elite of the elite of hard-core prisoners I was associating with. Absolutely anything could happen at any given moment, and I had to give the situation my undivided attention.

"My parole board hearing date was really kind of a joke anyway, considering that I had to be taken from solitary confinement to the hearing, and the reason I was in solitary confinement was for continually breaking prison rules and being disrespectful to the prison authorities. The way to get out of prison is to show remorse for your wrongdoing and be a well-behaved prisoner, but I had not done that, not by a long shot.

"Much to my surprise, a few weeks before my parole date a guard rapped on my cell and told me that we were going to the warden's office. That almost never happens. Most prisoners do their entire stretch without having a one-on-one with the warden. The only time I'd ever seen a warden was when they took me and my three Hell's Angels brothers to see the Vacaville warden when we arrived there.

"When we got to the warden's office he came out from behind the desk with a big white very official envelope in his hand and asked me if I knew anyone in the White House who might be sending me a letter. Yes, I did, I told him, and his name is Harold Pachios, at which point the warden took a letter out of the envelope and handed it to me. He had already read its contents, of course, that being the procedure with all prison mail.

"The letter was beautifully designed, with a finely-drawn picture of the White House up in the left hand corner, with '1600 Pennsylvania Avenue' under it, and Harold Pachios' name under that, all in raised gold-embossed lettering. The warden didn't give me a chance to read it in his presence, and I couldn't get much of a close-up look at it on the walk back to my cell, because my arms and wrists were shackled and I was in leg irons, but even from arm's length it looked like pretty interesting reading!

"Harold started the letter out with some words of

encouragement, because he'd do that kind of thing, but the important thing was that he said he was going to look into it. Guys like him don't just say things and then not do them, so all of a sudden I had a ray of hope.

"Not long after the letter arrived, I had a visit by a lawyer about my age who had gone to Princeton with Harold, and we hit it off very well. With the way I'd behaved since I was first arrested, though, I doubted very seriously that he could help me.

"There was a major consideration involved here. I told the lawyer that under no circumstance would I try to lay the blame for the suicide charge on my Hell's Angels brothers, and neither would I cast aspersions on my fellow inmates regarding activities I had been involved in since I had been in prison. I would provide absolutely no information for special favors. I hated snitches and rats then, and do to this day. So there would be no playing footsies with the parole board for me.

"When the day came the parole board treated me like royalty, though! I was completely blown away! All I heard from them was praise for staying out of jail all my life and for being an honorably discharged veteran! Not a word about the egregious nature of the suicide charge, and no mention of all the sorry bad-assed stuff I'd done during my period of incarceration! It was almost as if they were apologizing to me!

"They asked me to please take a seat out in the hall while my case was discussed, and when I came back in they told me that I was going to be paroled in ninety days!

"'What!?' I yelled!

"'You heard us right, Mr. Sawyer,' the chairman of the board said, 'and we certainly do hope that you appreciate your good fortune and will make the most of the opportunity to lead an honest, hard-working life from here on in.'"

"You're telling me that you were in San Quentin, looking at doing life in prison, then an acquaintance from your hometown intervened and you were released, just like that?" I said, with some skepticism in my voice.

"There's no way I can prove it to you," he said, "you'll just have to take my word for it."

"Yes, there's a way," I said, "I can call Harold Pachios and find out what he has to say about it."

"Harold wouldn't want anything to do with any of this, believe me," Jake responded. "He did me a huge favor, gave me back my life, actually, and I haven't done a very good job of justifying his faith in me since. No, as you will come to realize as time goes on, I have not led a very exemplary life since being paroled from San Quentin all those years ago, my friend, to say the very least. I have no doubt that the good gentleman deeply regrets his long-ago decision to help me. Let's just stay right away from him."

Up to this point, I'd been taking what Jake had been telling about himself as just that, but the prospect of some heavy-duty corroboration of his being paroled from San Quentin story was too enticing to pass up.

"I'd like to give him a call, Jake," I said. "You just never know."

He liked my tenacity. He knew I wouldn't have been as insistent with him about something when we first met, so he wanted to encourage my development as much as possible. He also couldn't say no to something as ballsy as contacting a very important man about something that happened almost fifty years ago, especially something that the man would have every reason to regret.

I knew Harold Pachios to be a well-known Portland attorney, and a founding partner of one of Portland's most prestigious law firms. He's also a popular host of a local radio program featuring discussions of the top social and political issues of the day. I wanted to know more about Mr. Pachios' background, though, so I Googled his name and discovered that his name is listed in Wood-White's 2015 edition of "The Best Lawyers in America", and that he was the Associated Press Secretary in the Lyndon Johnson White House in the late 1960s.

Truthfully, I didn't know if I could get the nerve up to call him. Powerful attorneys give me that same tightening in the stomach that being in Jake's presence once gave me. I did manage to work up the courage to call his office, though, and when the receptionist said Mr. Pachios was in and would take my call in just a moment, I knew all I could do was go for it, like Jake says you have to.

When Mr. Pachios picked up and I introduced myself and explained what I was calling about, he immediately said, "I've been following Jake's life story in *The Bollard* magazine and have been wondering if you were going to call me when you got to the San Quentin part!"

"Well, I didn't know if I, ah ..."

"Jake and I were brought up in the same neighborhood," he began. "I'm a couple of years older than Jake is, so we weren't boyhood friends, but we became acquainted over the years and I've always enjoyed chatting with him. He has an excellent reputation around the old neighborhood. He was a big kid, because he lifted weights, and he liked to fight, but he wasn't a bully. He'd only fight with other kids who liked to fight, or he'd beat up guys who picked on the smaller kids.

"He's a very talented and intelligent guy, that I can tell you. And he has a terrific sense of humor. I know he's done a lot of jail time since I helped him get paroled from San Quentin. Of course, I don't condone the things he's done, but he's always been straight with me.

"I'd been following his career, from knowing his family, and in the media, so I was very interested when I saw the letter from him on my desk in my office at the White House. I was the Associated Press Secretary under Lyndon Johnson at the time, and my office was just down the hall from the Oval Office. Jake's letter got a lot of notice when it arrived because of his very large and kind of ornate handwriting, and the mysterious return address of Tamal, California. One of the secretaries looked it up, and there is no such place, but we found out later that Tamal is a special return address for San Quentin."

Wait a minute, here, I thought. This man remembers the return address on the envelope from almost fifty years ago? Ah, the rewards of a life well spent.

"I was very surprised to get a letter from Jake, of course. To tell you the truth, I didn't even know that he was in San Quentin, and I was intrigued by the fact that he was even writing to me, so I sent him a letter telling him that I was going to look into the matter. Then after I found out a little bit about what was going on, I called an attorney friend who I went to Princeton with and who had recently joined a San Francisco law firm. He visited with Jake at San Quentin a few times and evidently they got along very well because my friend ended up spending a lot of time on Jake's case, even though he was practicing as an environmental lawyer, not as a criminal lawyer.

"My surmise is that the State of California came to see that Jake's case had the potential of becoming the undoing of the 'Five Years to Life' program. Here we had a man with no priors, having not murdered anyone or stolen a lot of money, who's headed for spending life in prison with hardened criminals, mainly because he can't behave in prison. And the man's a Hell's Angel, to top it off. Governor Reagan did not want Jake to become a folk hero and then have to deal with demonstrators outside the prison, so better to wipe his hands clean of it all and set him free. An option made all the more attractive by the arrival of a letter to the subject from a man whose office was two doors down from Lyndon Johnson's."

I asked Mr. Pachios if I could quote him in this story and he said, "Yeah, go ahead! Jake's always been an up-front guy as far as I'm concerned. He has a great sense of fairness about him, and loyalty to his friends. He did me a great favor once. It was sort of payback, I guess, but I had the feeling that he would have done it for me even if he didn't owe me a favor."

"A favor?" I asked.

"When I left the White House, President Johnson gave me a pair of gold cuff links with the Presidential Seal on the front and 'LBJ' on the back as a memento of our time in the White House together, and when I returned to Portland and was checking into the Eastland Hotel someone rifled through my luggage in my car parked out front and stole them. I was distressed because they meant a lot to me. I knew it was very unlikely that the police were going to make that kind of recovery, so I called Jake and asked him if he would see what he could do. He didn't sound too hopeful, but he told me he'd try. I really didn't expect to hear from him, and I said I'd certainly understand if I didn't, but a couple of weeks later he called me and asked me where I wanted the cuff links dropped off. Recovering those cuff links meant an awful lot to me, believe me. I wear them a couple of times a year now, on special occasions, and I invariably smile and think of Jake as I'm putting them on."

"Good-bye, Harold," I said, "Jake will be delighted when I tell him about our conversation."

Jake was indeed delighted. Very delighted.

Jake, friend Eddie Griffin (owner of the Griffin Club Tavern), and attorney Harold Pachios

JAKE

The document granting Jake parole from San Quentin. Jake says he chuckles, even after all these years, whenever he reads the "GO TO MAINE" typed in capital letters because it makes him recall how furious the prison authorities were to see him paroled and how intent they were on his leaving California immediately, if not sooner.

ELEVEN

W hen I called to discuss where we should meet this time, in his apartment or elsewhere, Jake immediately said he'd prefer the Munjoy Hill Tavern. I knew he didn't care about drinking beer, and now that we were moving on from talking about the Hell's Angels, I thought we'd be meeting elsewhere, most likely in his apartment, so I was a little surprised when he said he wanted to go back to the tavern.

"I feel very comfortable at Stan's place. Our little project has come to mean a great deal to him, too, you know."

Indeed. Little lights had started to go on for me the last couple of times Jake and I got together at the tavern. Stan was like the guy in the corridor of Jake's building, the woman in the elevator, the imperious seagull out on the ledge, and me. We're all Jake's friends. Just like the Regulators were at San Quentin, not to mention the honorable Harold Pachios, who ultimately played such a part in delivering Jake from the mess he was in. Jake's our friend and we are his friends.

When we arrived at the tavern, Stan was behind the bar doing some book work, which he immediately set aside when he saw us.

"Stan!" Jake yelled. "Get yourself a beer too and come and join us!"

"No, no," Stan demurred, "I don't want to bother you guys. I just want to see you get this book done!"

"You got it, man!" Jake yelled, "watch for *JAKE* at your favorite bookstore very, very soon!"

"Okay, Jake," I said, getting right to what had been on my mind, after we were seated at our usual table out in the backyard. "So, Jake, did your outlook on life change significantly after you got so miraculously paroled from San Quentin? Damn, you'd been in prison for a little over two years, total, and you were looking at the possibly never getting out alive!"

"Damn! I don't know about changing my outlook, but I sure as hell felt great! I felt like a majestic bird who had gotten trapped in a trash bag and finally got out! I did that for a blackbird once, saw the bag thrashing around, you know. I'll never forget him swooping up into the sky when he got out, screeching his heart out with the pure joy of it! And that was me the day I got out of San Quentin!"

"So after you got paroled from San Quentin, you went right straight home to Portland, married your high school sweetheart, got a job selling life insurance, bought a nice home in South Portland, and got active in the Chamber of Commerce, right?"

He laughed as hard as I've ever seen him laugh.

"Stan!" he yelled. "Come throw this guy out! He's had too much to drink!"

Stan poked his head around the corner, checking to be sure Jake was just joking, and it occurred to me that it was fortunate for me that he was.

"Alright, Jake, calm down, there's no need to call in the infantry," I said, "just tell me what was going on inside your head when you got released from San Quentin. Damn! You'd been given your life back! How did you feel about getting such a huge break out of nowhere when you knew damn well you didn't deserve it? Talk about getting a second chance! Did you have any grand resolutions about how you were going to live the rest of your life now that you had it handed back to you?"

He looked over at me with his mouth hanging open

for what seemed like a very long time, as if he was completely baffled by what he had just heard me ask him and had no idea how to respond. Then he exploded.

"You haven't understood a damn thing about anything I've been telling you all this time! Haven't you gotten to know what I'm like at all?! Second chances?! Grand resolutions?! What the hell kind of language are you speaking?! That shit does not apply to me! I had no fucking intention of changing one fucking thing about myself because I knew I couldn't change who I am even if I had wanted to!"

Okay, I thought to myself as I sat there calmly looking over at him, maybe I'll try asking him questions having to do with inner reflection and personal growth a little later, if the occasion arises. For the moment, though, I thought it might be better to go for a blow by blow account of how his release day went.

"Excuse me for that eruption, my friend," he said, "sometimes I get a little too rambunctious, if you haven't noticed. Let me calm down a bit and address your initial question, then I'll give you a thorough accounting of the events that took place at the time of my release.

"First, I'll address your question concerning the effect that the good fortune I experienced had on me. I felt a deep gratitude to the people, especially Harold Pachios, who helped get me out of San Quentin, yes, of course I did, but I was not obligated to change my life for them. That was something I just couldn't do, even if I had wanted to. There actually was a part of me that wanted to go straight, I guess. Sometimes when I reflected on how I had lived my life, I could see a little neglected child whimpering in the background, and I know that was my gentle, peaceful self, but that wasn't, and isn't, who I really am, not by a long shot. Who I am is an extremely dangerous character focused on dominating any situation I find myself in, by violent means if necessary. I also have a deep-rooted love for my fellow man, though.

"Now as to the events surrounding my release, which are indelibly etched in my memory, my friend, and which I would be happy to relate to you.

"There is no way I can describe for you how it felt to look out my cell window watching the sun come up on the morning of my release date. June, 17, 1968! Ah! The long-awaited day had arrived!

"There it was, glistening off in the distance! Oakland, California! Where the clubhouse of the Hell's Angels Motorcycle Club was located!

"At about eight in the morning, a guard showed up and escorted me to Receiving and Release, where you are issued some civilian clothes, get fifty dollars, as I remember, and sign some papers. The best thing I could find in the clothing room was a comically out-of-style blue suit, a white shirt that was a couple of sizes too big for me, and an ugly necktie. The attending guards made a big joke of saying over and over how great I looked, and I laughed like hell about it right along with them. Most of the guards were okay guys, just doing their jobs. There were a few maggots among them, like there are wherever you go, but we'll get to how I dealt with those guys a little later.

"After I got my fifty dollars cash and my snappy new duds, I was standing at the Receiving and Release window putting the dough in my wallet when a door opened behind me. As I looked over my shoulder to see who was coming in, one of the guards nodded his head at the door, by way of indicating that it was open for me to go out. You have no idea what it means to someone who hasn't walked through an open door to the outside for two years. What an overwhelming feeling of joy came over me as I stepped out and calmly closed that door behind me. There I was, outside in the open air, all alone, with no one standing next to me, behind me or in front of me. The things in life we take for granted, man!

"As I walked down the half-mile long sidewalk that leads from the main prison to the guard shack at the San Quentin Prison entry gate, I swung my head from side to side, looking up into the sky all around me, just taking it in. When you've only seen the sky from a walled-in prison yard for as long as I had, the open sky is a wonderful sight and the air smells like a field of flowers.

"Needless to say, the parole board placed some very strict limitations and conditions on my release. To begin with, they said I had to be out of the State of California within twenty-four hours and immediately get headed back to Maine, where I needed to report to my parole officer within seven days after my release, which would have made my report date June 24th.

"To say that the authorities were something less than happy with my sudden early release would be a gross understatement. They were absolutely furious, actually. The warden said that it was pure lunacy to release an unrepentant, violent criminal from prison after having served such a short amount of time as I had, especially in light of the fact that said prisoner had made no effort to abide by prison rules.

"The scuttlebutt was that Governor Ronald Reagan was beside himself with fury at my release. His 'Five years to Life' program was the central part of the law and order platform he had run on for governor, and he apparently was very disturbed when he heard that an official in Lyndon Johnson's White House had meddled in a matter that he considered to be strictly an affair of the State of California. 'Damn those Democrats!' I could almost hear him sputtering. He probably decided to run for President at that point, you never know. He owes it all to me! Hey, Don't mention it, Ronnie!

"In addition to having to immediately return to Maine, I also had to agree to undergo extensive psychiatric therapy when I arrived home in Portland, the purpose of which would be to bring about an extreme modification of my behavior, the parole board said. I readily agreed to all the conditions they set, of course, but they were somewhat skeptical of my sincerity. The last thing the warden said to me as I walked out of his office was that he would be seeing me again if I so much as spit on the sidewalk. I very politely told him that I'd never do such a thing, it wasn't my style, so he didn't have to worry. He didn't respond, but he did smile and give me one of those 'bye bye, see you soon' little waves. I always knew he was a nice guy at heart.

"I was absolutely determined to prove him wrong, though. Hey, I'd be a complete phony if I told you that I was any less than ecstatic at being out of prison. You might have noticed somewhere along the line here that I'm absolutely in love with life and have a great passion for taking in huge gulps of excitement whenever the opportunity presents itself. At first, I wasn't at all upset about being incarcerated because I've always thrived in an all-male environment, especially one in which violence is the order of the day. I'm an adrenalin junkie all the way, and being in the company of the toughest, meanest criminals in the entire country had me alert and on my game, big time. Truthfully, I've never felt more alive than when I first went to San

Quentin. I didn't have a moment to feel sorry for myself, or to give any thought to what I was missing on the outside, even though I had been getting laid by some of the most beautiful women in California. That's how intense my involvement in life on the inside was. That's the secret of serving time in a prison, as I have told you. Get your mind off the outside and live your life totally according to your present reality.

"But after I had taken matters into my own hands and risen to the top of the heap in prison, the thrill was gone, and all I could think of was how the hell I was going to get out of there. It also didn't help that, regardless of my stature within the prison population, chances were very good that I was going to end up on a prison floor with a shank driven into me.

"Oh what a feeling it was to step into that cab parked at the main gate, take that wonderful ride to the Greyhound bus station in Oakland and board that bus to Sacramento!

"My plan was to pick up the dark blue 1964 Chevy Supersport car my good friend Pete Hill was storing for me. He and his wife Jeanne had spent a lot of time camping out in Maine, so we bonded right away when we met in California. Pete said he never had any doubt that I'd be by before long to pick the car up. I stood up and walked across the room and shook his hand when he said that, and I have often thought of that moment over the years. Pete and Jeanne had a fantastic steak dinner waiting for me when I arrived, with some great Colorado pot and California wine to go with it. It was my first night of freedom, man, and we did it up big. Some evenings stay with you forever, and that's one of them for me. Pete even gave me $1000 cash and said I didn't have to worry about paying him back until sometime in the future when I could afford to.

JAKE

"Bright and early the next morning, I said good-bye to Pete and Jeanne and drove to Sonny Barger's beautiful home in Oakland. When I pulled up, Sonny was in his garage working on his new Harley and was very happy to see me. We met halfway up his driveway and he gave me a big hug. Man, I was levitated with joy!

"Sonny made a few calls to our Hell's Angels brothers and they started showing up throughout the day and night. Man, did we party! Terry the Tramp arrived driving a late model Jaguar Xke convertible, with a Bob Dylan song turned up full blast. Janis Joplin was obsessed with him and she bought the Jaguar for him, and he thought I'd like to see it. Terry and I were so happy to see each other we danced around together laughing our heads off pounding each other on the back on and off all afternoon.

"Just for the record, my friend," Jake continued, "the name of the young lady Sonny sent to visit me when I was first incarcerated at San Quentin was Ginger, and when I got miraculously paroled from San Quentin she was waiting for me at Sonny's house! We spent the night in his bed, and I've always considered that to be one of the highest honors I have ever received in my life. You might also be interested in knowing that Ginger was a part-time girlfriend of Terry the Tramp, who had a lot of part-time girl-friends. Ginger was a UCLA graduate and was attract-ed to college educated Hell's Angels like Terry and me. Janis Joplin hated her, of course, because of Terry. Ginger even came from Oakland to visit me in Portland a few times after I returned home, then after a while she'd go back to Terry.

"The party at Sonny's house lasted for two whole glorious days and nights, in spite of the fact that the parole board had given me twenty-four hours to be out of the State of California. Leaving the state without saying my proper good-byes to my Hell's Angels brothers and spending quality time with Ginger was just not going to happen, though."

PEACE AND LOVE

"There's no question that my forced separation from my Hell's Angels brothers had been bearing down heavily on me, but I knew I was still a Hell's Angels Nomad in the very best of standing in the club.

"There I was, free, with my whole life in front of me. From being in solitary confinement at San Quentin to being out on the open highway traveling across America at a very high rate of speed in a very cool car was almost too much for me to take in. My head was whirling and I was happy as hell!

"Free! There I was, tooling along a highway in New Mexico on a beautiful June day, free, free, free, when out of nowhere I spotted a young couple hitchhiking and picked them up. The woman had flowers in her hair, he had a red bandanna around his head, and neither of them was wearing shoes. When they got in the car there was this cloud of what I later knew to be patchouli perfume that accompanied them, and now I had my introduction to hippies. The whole hippie thing happened when I was incarcerated, you see, so I had no idea what they were all about. I was very intrigued, though.

"They told me that they were going to a hippie wedding in the mountains, which was taking place on June 21 because it is the first day of summer and the longest day of the year, and asked me if I wanted to come along. Hey, why not, I thought, I've got the time."

Well, not really, but whatever, I was thinking.

"When their hippie friends saw me step out of the car wearing my full Hell's Angels regalia they started cheering! The Hell's Angels were folk heroes to them, and they were absolutely thrilled to have me in their presence. They treated me like I was some kind of royalty. Right away they started handing me joints and multiple hits of LSD and ka-zoom! I was in heaven!

"They formed a circle around a tepee they had set up in the middle of a large clearing and held hands as they danced around it, with the happy hippie couple consummating their love inside. It was a sight to behold, especially for someone who had been in prison for as long as I had been. They all had colorful streamers they were waving over their heads as they danced around the tepee, and everyone was high as hell on life itself and on every drug there was.

"Guess what?! My ol' buddy Allen Ginsburg was there!

"Of course, he recognized me right away from when I met him at Sonny's house, soon after I had made the acquaintance of my Hell's Angels brothers. Unfortunately, Neil Cassidy, who I also met at Sonny's, had passed away in the meantime, and Allen appreciated my extending my regrets. We also chatted a bit about Bob Dylan having recently gotten into an accident riding his Triumph. We were concerned for him, of course. We also knew he wasn't a very skilled motorcyclist because of his poor eyesight. Allen also asked me about how Terry the Tramp really felt about Janis Joplin but, naturally, I didn't share a thing with him about that. I am not a rat, in any way, whether the subject involves the law or the personal life of a friend.

"All this happy hippie stuff went on for three days. Oh, I almost forgot, I consummated my relationship with a couple of hippie girls in the tepee, in keeping with the happy occasion, you know, and on the morning of the third day I lit out for Maine."

Okay, I said to myself, now we're at June 24, which is the day he was supposed to report to his parole officer in Portland. I'm sure the hippie wedding was fun, but was it worth being sent back to prison, maybe never to see the light of day again? I asked him.

"You've got a good point there," he said, "after the hippie wedding, I got right back on the highway and headed back to Maine ... oh, no, wait ... I did stop along the Colorado River to visit Hoover Dam. I just had to. It was almost on the way home, you know? What a wondrous sight it was too! I was mesmerized by all that power and energy in one place!"

He took time for sightseeing when he was already running very late?

THE HAPPY TOURIST

"While I was on the tour of Hoover Dam, I thought I'd send some picture postcards to the guards at San Quentin who had screwed me over in one way or another. 'This is where your mother and me are shacked up' was one of the greetings I wrote in big bold letters in the space for cheery hellos. I came up with a few other friendly messages that were equally as charming, but I knew that my contempt for them didn't matter to them in the slightest, of course. I'm sure they got together and laughed like hell about the postcards. Hey, they were only doing their jobs, even if some of them were assholes. I guess the time I had just spent with the hippies mellowed me out a little, after all, and I wanted to do something nice for someone.

"After I had taken in the Hoover Dam and attended to the social niceties just referred to, I was off and running, headed straight back to Maine. It was now June 26 and I was already two days late for my appointment with my parole officer in Portland. I had gotten only as far as Colorado, so, of course, I was in an awful rush to get back home.

A BRIEF STOP IN THE COMBAT ZONE

"After barreling across America just about non-stop, I was only about five days late for the appointment with my parole officer in Portland when I got to Massachusetts, so when I was on the highway outside of Boston I decided to take a little detour. About a forty mile one, actually. I just had to pay a visit to the Combat Zone, where I was sure I'd run into some old friends.

"It was nighttime when I arrived in the Combat Zone. I parked my car on Washington Street, right across from Jerome's, which you will remember was on street level, just under the Mid-City Health Club, now shuttered and looking forlorn due to my absence.

"Man, had things changed at the Novelty Bar across Beach Street, where I used to hang out! Unbeknownst to me, the place was now an outlaw-biker bar. As I stepped through the door, wearing my full Hell's Angels regalia, I saw about two dozen bikers sitting at tables and standing around wearing the insignia of an outlaw-biker club named the Devil's Disciples. They had formed during my time away and I had never heard of them, but I got to know them very quickly.

"When they saw a Hell's Angels Nomad walk into their bar, they immediately glared at me like I was going to be a dead man very soon. I knew, of course, what was up and I would've turned around and walked out had that been an option, but they would've chased me down anyway, so, I just threw up my arms and yelled, 'Hi, guys!'

"My haughty attitude incited them to violence, big time, as I damn well knew it would, and before I could even reach inside my jacket and pull out the finely sharpened hunting knife I always carried, they were on me and there I was, at the bottom of a pile of furious Devil's Disciples.

"That there were so many of them turned out to be to my advantage because they couldn't get by one another to get a good swing at me. Some of them were on the edges of the pile kicking at me, but they couldn't get in any good kicks because of all the bodies on top of me, and ones on top of me couldn't get in any good punches because of all the congestion. I knew they'd get it all sorted out soon enough and I'd be dog meat when they did. But, once again in my life, my guardian angel made her appearance. The whole pile of sweaty bodies suddenly shifted, and I saw daylight, and I managed to get free of the whole mess.

"Somehow or other, in all the confusion, I squirmed out from underneath the pile and headed for a side door, but there was a big fat mean looking Devil's Disciple blocking it. I punched him very viciously in the face, and that pretty much took care of him, but the delay enabled one of the others to catch up to me and slash the back of my right hand with a broken beer bottle.

"At the moment he did it, I didn't realize the extent of the injury and just kept heading for the door, which opened up onto an alley. A number of Devil's Disciples followed me up the alley, of course, with the full intent of slicing me up like a Boston scrod and stuffing me in a garbage can. There was no doubt they were going to catch me because a couple others had gone out the front door and were blocking the end of the alley that emptied out on the sidewalk, but out of nowhere a squadron of Boston finest came to my rescue.

"The Boston police had what they called a 'goon squad,' which was made up of the biggest and toughest guys on the police force, and they just happened to be cruising by in a squad car just as me and my pursuers were coming up the alley. As soon as the Devil's Disciples spotted them they backed off because they knew if they didn't they'd all be carried off in paddy wagons if they had persisted in their mission.

"So, I was safe, but at that point I fully realized the extent of the damage to my right hand, and I immediately jumped in my car and headed to Mass General Hospital. This was not at all the homecoming I had expected to take place in the Combat Zone, and I was quite dismayed at it all."

MASS GENERAL HOSPITAL

"When I arrived at the emergency room of Mass General, the first thing the doctors wanted to do was put me to sleep, but I would have none of that. They were in utter disbelief, but I persisted in my madness. What they didn't get was that I was certain that while

I was out they were going to call the police, because it was obvious that I had been in a fight. Calling the police meant that I'd be sent back to San Quentin for a parole violation, and, like the warden said, I'd never get out of the place. I also knew that the Devil's Disciples might well have followed me to the hospital, and that the first thing they would do while I was out would be to steal my 'colors.' It would have been a grand coup for them to have the Hell's Angels colors in their possession, particularly the colors of a Hell's Angels Nomad, and the fact that they would have to invade the emergency room of Mass General Hospital would have been no deterrence at all for them.

"The doctors examined my hand and told me that all the tendons across the back of my hand, just above the knuckles, had been severed all the way through, and that I'd need extensive surgery to save the hand.

"The long and short of it is that I told the doctors that I wouldn't allow them to even touch me if they insisted on putting me out, because I was an orphan who had been raised by the Shaker community in New Gloucester, Maine, and Shakers don't take medication for pain, so they agreed to operate on me without putting me out.

"One of the nurses was from Maine, and when no one else was around she came over to me and said, 'So you're a Hell's Angel from California and you were brought up by the Shakers in Sabathday Lake, Maine, huh?'

"'Sure!' I said, and we both cracked up.

"There I was, in the operation room wearing a johnny over my Hell's Angels colors, with a silly-assed look on my face. I knew she felt bad for me, but she couldn't help giggling every time she walked by.

"I did, of course, receive a number of shots of a local

anesthetic, I like to think of myself as being a big tough guy, in case you weren't aware of that, but the operation was so excruciatingly painful that tears flowed from my eyes very freely, even with the anesthetic shots I was given. It was purely physical reaction to the pain I was experiencing. I managed not to cry out, though. I knew that if I did that my objection to them putting me out would be over-ridden.

"The ordeal lasted for over two hours, and they were two of the most memorable hours of my life. Well, now, of course, we have to remember that I had been through this kind of horseshit before, after having my right leg almost completely torn off in my motorcycle accident a few years before, but that didn't make this time any easier. Anybody who tells you that they've become immune to pain because they've had so much of it in the past is talking through their ass. And the pain wasn't restricted to just my hand, either. My whole arm ached like hell and there was pulsating pain up to my neck and across my entire back. I sat there staring at the ceiling thinking about my mother and how gently she'd put a bandage on my finger when I got a little cut when I was a kid. Can a man own up to that kind of thing and still be a man? I don't know, but there it is.

"After the ordeal was over, they put me in a room by myself to rest a little, but I knew I had to get out of there before the Devil's Disciples showed up. I also had to get to Portland because by this time I was already six days late reporting to my parole officer. So, after spotting the little nurse from Maine in the corridor and whispering to her that I was headed back to Maine to rejoin the Shaker community, I was out of there and back in my cool car for the hundred-mile ride up the turnpike to Portland, ready to get on with the rest of my life."

He was now six days late reporting to his parole officer. What other risks would this guy take while getting on with the rest of his life? I didn't know, but I was very eager to find out.

Jake's story continues in

Volume Two of *JAKE*

**THE RIDE'S NOT OVER YET!
NOT BY A LONG SHOT!**

**VOLUME TWO OF "JAKE" IS
WHERE THINGS REALLY
START TO GET CRAZY!**

**SO HANG ON AND LEAN
INTO THE CURVES!**

Volume One and Volume Two are
available online at Amazon.com!